The
Southern Way

The regular volume for the Southern devotee

Kevin Robertson

Issue 39

www.crecy.co.uk

© 2017 Crécy Publishing Ltd
and the various contributors

ISBN 9781909328631

First published in 2017 by Noodle Books
an imprint of Crécy Publishing Ltd

All editorial submissions to:
The Southern Way (Kevin Robertson)
Conway
Warnford Rd
Corhampton
Hants SO32 3ND
Tel: 01489 877880
editorial@thesouthernway.co.uk

Publisher's note: Every effort has been made to identify and correctly attribute photographic credits. Any error that may have occurred is entirely unintentional.
In line with the new design the front cover image has changed from that originally advertised. All other information is unaffected.

Printed in Malta by Melita Press

Noodle Books is an imprint of
Crécy Publishing Limited
1a Ringway Trading Estate
Shadowmoss Road
Manchester M22 5LH

www.crecy.co.uk

Issue No 40 of THE SOUTHERN WAY
ISBN 9781909328648
available in October 2017 at £14.95
To receive your copy the moment it is released, order in advance from your usual supplier, or it can be sent post-free (UK) direct from the publisher:

Crécy Publishing Ltd

1a Ringway Trading Estate, Shadowmoss Road, Manchester M22 5LH

Tel 0161 499 0024

www.crecy.co.uk

enquiries@crecy.co.uk

Front Cover:
Typifying the end at Nine Elms (even if it was taken some time in the autumn of 1966). Rebuilt 'Merchant Navy' No 35029 *Ellerman Lines* stands cold and forlorn at Nine Elms awaiting what at the time seemed an inevitable future – scrap. Erected at Eastleigh and entering traffic in February 1949, the engine had a life of 10 years before being rebuilt in the form seen in the summer of 1959. A Nine Elms engine from 1955 until 1964, it spent its final years in traffic based at Weymouth, until it was withdrawn having run a recorded mileage of 748,343 miles in total. Clearly seen stored at Nine Elms, it was later moved to store at Weymouth, where it remained until April 1967, after which it resided at Barry awaiting what appeared to be an inevitable fate. Chance, though, would now play its hand, for No 35029 was selected for preservation (of sorts) but as a sectioned exhibit for the National Collection intended to demonstrate how a steam locomotive was constructed and worked. In consequence the engine was moved from Barry to (it is thought) Sewstern, on the ex-British Steel iron-ore quarry line at the end of the High Dyke branch south of Grantham. Here, within the confines of the former British Steel workshop, the right-hand side of the cab, firebox, boiler, smokebox, right-hand cylinder and framing were cut away to reveal the 'inner workings'. (See http://www.flickr.com/photos/davidwf2009/collections/72157626274215250/)

A Bulleid tender was similarly sectioned. Contemporary press records reported the then privately owned Flying Scotsman Enterprises had been involved in the work. The final touches were to restore cosmetically No 35029 and tender, after which they were placed on permanent display at the National Railway Museum, where the engine continues to reside. Alongside No 35029, Class 4 tank engine No 80095 had similarly been withdrawn in October 1966.

Rear Cover:
One to indeed end with. LBSCR 10T round-ended wagon, later to SR Diagram 1369, LBSCR No 4333, later SR 23216, renumbered at Lancing in December 1925. Recorded on the Corringham Light Railway, Essex, in 1920. *With grateful thanks to Mike King (LGRP)*

Title page:
Happier times. No 35029 at the head of a diverted Bournemouth line train passing Ropley in January 1961 with the diverted 10.30 down. *John Bailey*

Contents

Editorial

For this issue we welcome another guest editor, Chris Sayers-Leavy, with his piece entitled 'Looking back – with the benefit of hindsight ...'

First, I am grateful to Kevin Robertson for being given the opportunity to pen these lines. Since I retired some three years ago now from the post of a senior engineer with Network Rail, I have had the time to indulge myself (as one might expect) in various things that interest me. Being a lifelong follower of the development and use of most things that are/were steam driven, and railways in particular, I find that it has been all too easy for me to adopt an 'affiliation' for a particular style of engineering and railway operations. Whether by intention or design, the 'Big Four' companies, prior to nationalisation, seemed to cultivate a style in their own individual ways. I suppose that this affiliation is a bit like supporting a football team; you pick a team to support when you are a youngster and you inevitably stay with that team, through thick and thin, no matter what – all of your life. However, for me, the parallels end here as I was never a football (or for that matter any other form of sports) fan.

Having also lived for most of my life in the South Eastern quarter of the UK, I am somewhat naturally drawn to the activities of the former Southern Railway, its foregoing companies and subsequently the post nationalisation activities of the Southern Region of British Railways/British Rail right up to the industry privatisation in 1994. I must admit that I also quite admire the old Southern's 'make do and mend/re-use' philosophy – for whatever reason it pervaded – and of course longevity is a feature of railway engineering, things were built to last and last they did. It might even be said that on some occasions this rebuilding and reuse of equipment and stock lasted too long but by so doing they did at least provide a good value return on the initial investment.

So where, you might be thinking, is this rambling trail of thought going? Well, the 'status quo' as it was, carried on down the years until a certain Mr O. V. S. Bulleid appeared on the scene and then there was a major departure from all that had gone before and which for me commences a period of great interest. Like him or loathe him, Bulleid was very much a 'one off' and the usual *Southern Way* editor has indeed written at length about the man and his machines down the years.

However, partly no doubt due to my engineering background, I find myself drawn to his engineering innovations, ideas and designs, some of which were in my opinion very good, whilst others were 'dead ends' and probably should never have been allowed to have started. But of course, unless you try out a new idea you will just never know what the outcome will be and things will not change at all – unless that is you make it happen ...

This, then, is how the title of this text arises, as I find myself making personal judgements on Bulleid's activities, all these years later, not, I will admit, based on first-hand knowledge and experience but very much with the benefit of *hindsight* – something which in many ways is all too easily done.

Personally, I well recall the last days of steam on the Southern (quite rightly being recounted in this publication) and watching the Bulleid machines on the South Western main line. In many ways they were very impressive, but I come to ask myself, how did the designer of these engines also make the mistakes that he did? This, then, is the paradox.

As with everything else in life, time now passes by seemingly at an ever increasing pace and many of those people that were around at the time of Bulleid's tenure are no longer with us and so unable to give some insight into what made him 'tick'. I was, however, fortunate to have been involved in the initial return to steam of 'West Country' No 21C123 *Blackmoor Vale* on the Bluebell Railway and this gave me the opportunity to take a close look at some of the design features. In many ways, to me at least, a number of his ideas could be seen to be destined to fail from the outset, but of course this is (at the risk of repeating myself) 'with the benefit of *hindsight*'. Thus I try to take as much of an 'objective' view of Bulleid's 'engineering' as I can, that is before starting to be critical, but we must also not forget that the world was a very different place 75 years or so ago when said designer dared to think outside of the box. Consequently it is essential we ensure we keep current-day comments and observations in context with the period during which the events happened and the machines were constructed. Suffice to say, that it would be impossible today to get away with some of the things that used to go on on the railway all those years ago ...

Chris Sayers-Leavy

If you would like to contribute in similar fashion why not drop us a line. The topic is to your choice and with very limited restrictions. Steam, electric, diesel – Southern related of course – lines, Southern or BRS policies or politics even. The only proviso being that we will not allow discussion on politics relevant to the current rail operators. This is your choice to comment on what has been done or perhaps should have been done; we look forward to hearing from you. I cannot promise vast sums of remuneration but you will at least receive a free copy of the relevant issue.

Kevin Robertson

S. W. Milford – A Lifetime of LSWR Service

The *Southern Railway Magazine* included in its 1924 issue a portrait and brief biography of Mr S. W. Milford, who had retired from the position of District Superintendent of Central District of the Southern Railway (SR) and previously of the London & South Western Railway (LSWR) at Southampton on 31 December 1923.

With the SR and its antecedents having employed thousands of men, such an entry might, in the normal course of events, be simply passed over with a brief read through and the inevitable short ponder – 'who' and 'what stories might he have been able to tell'?

At this point I now need to revert back a few years; not, I will admit, to anything like the 90-plus years since Mr Milford's retirement but instead to the early days of SW and when some kind hearted soul passed me a file marked 'S. W. Milford' and which after several years I have at last got around to reading.

Let it also be said straightaway, this is not, sadly, another summary of the life of a senior Southern Railway officer as we had recently with Charles Anderson. Indeed, I am ashamed to admit I have singularly failed to even ascribe to what the initials 'S. W.' relate to. What we have instead, though, are various notes and correspondence referring to what must have been specific instances in a career that occupied 45 years, commencing as a junior clerk in the divisional traffic superintendent's office, an office then under the charge of Mr J. Tyler. (In 1924 it was reported that Mr Tyler – junior – was then assistant to the Chief Engineer at Waterloo.) Following his initial clerical post, Mr Milford gained experience in several areas before progressing to the post of chief clerk and acting assistant to the divisional superintendent at Exeter.

During the tenure of S. W. Milford at Exeter, trains between Exeter and Waterloo would have passed through Winchfield station in the form it is seen here – two platforms and a down siding (later a down loop), seen looking east (up) towards Fleet and Waterloo. The horse is standing in the up siding looking towards where a wagon turntable was located with two sidings at 90° to the left. According to the George Pryer signal box diagrams, a signal box had been provided at the east end of the station from 1875 onwards, after which we might expect to see signals at the end of the platform in the position of the water cranes plus several ground signals. Their absence would therefore tend to date the view prior to 1875.

S. W. Milford.

Progression now took him via Eastleigh to Southampton as the district superintendent in place of Mr A. H. Wadden. His tenure here certainly included the difficult days of World War 1, for which services he was awarded an OBE.

This, then, is the limit of factual information, as per the 1924 SR magazine entry which was accompanied by a small portrait. However, the file referred to earlier does provide a teasing glimpse of his work activities, all contained in a somewhat battered paper folio entitled 'Miscellaneous Memoranda'. Milford, it appears, retained this file as a record of what was taking place when and where he was employed and includes some fascinating information about the development and operation of the railways west of Exeter, some of which were still being developed post-1878 – the year he had commenced at Exeter. There is, for example, an undated statement of maximum loads for goods trains in the Western District running to several pages in faded copperplate containing the information shown below:

From	To	Loads (vehicles) Passenger or mixed traffic engine	Loads (vehicles) Goods Engine	Remarks
Yeovil and Exeter line, down through fast trains				
Yeovil Junction	Exeter	30	35	
Yeovil and Exeter line, down stopping trains				
Yeovil Junction	Crewkerne	30	40	
Chard Junction	Axminster	40	40	
Axminster	Honiton	30	35	
Honiton	Exeter	35	45	
Yeovil and Exeter line, up through fast trains				
Exeter	Yeovil Junction		35	8.00 pm Market Train is limited to 29 vehicles and 9.50 pm to 30. Cattle specials to 30 and 2 vans.
Yeovil and Exeter line, up stopping trains				
Exeter	Honiton	35	35	
Honiton	Crewkerne	40	40	
Crewkerne	Yeovil Junction	50	50	
Exeter and Plymouth line, down through fast trains				
Exeter	Devonport	25	25	
Devonport	Friary	40	40	
Exeter and Plymouth line, down stopping trains				
Exeter Queen Street	St Davids	43	43	
Exeter St Davids	Yeoford	50	50	Except the 2.35 am which is limited to 35 vehicles.
Yeoford	Bridestowe	27	30	
Bridestowe	Tavistock	40	40	
Tavistock	Bere Alston	30	35	
Bere Alston	Friary	40	40	
Exeter and Plymouth line, up trains				
Friary	Devonport	30	30	Except 6.20 pm which is limited to 20.
Devonport	Okehampton	30	30	30 is considered a load for mixed wagons but when a train made up of wagons loaded from the various docks, 25 should be the maximum. The 3.45 am newspaper train for Devonport, on account of it being subsidised by the newspaper proprietors, is limited to 16 vehicles only, it being timed sharp.
Okehampton	Crediton	40	40	Except 6.30 pm fast which is limited to 30 between Okehampton and Exeter.

From	To	Loads (vehicles) Passenger or mixed traffic engine	Loads (vehicles) Goods Engine	Remarks
Crediton	Exeter	40	40	Except 3.45 am ex Torrington which is limited to 35. Goods trains heavy with coal load to be limited to 30. The 9.15 and 9.40 pm trains from Friary must not exceed 30 vehicles, there being only two engines available to take the trains up the incline from St Davids to Queen Street. On Sundays the load of the 2.40 am train from North Road is limited to 20 vehicles from Yeoford, and the 12.30 pm train from Friary is limited to 20 from Crediton to avoid the necessity of a second engine being provided from St Davids to Queen Street.

North Devon line, down trains

From	To	Loads (vehicles) Passenger or mixed traffic engine	Loads (vehicles) Goods Engine	Remarks
Yeoford	Barnstaple	40	40	The 2.35 pm Mail from Exeter is limited to 35 vehicles. The 10.47 am stopping train from Exeter can take 50 vehicles from Yeoford to Copplestone and 60 beyond.
Barnstaple	Fremington	50	50	One man trains
Barnstaple	Fremington	60	60	Two man trains
Fremington	Bideford	40	40	One man trains
Fremington	Bideford	50	50	Two man trains
Bideford	Torrington	35	35	

North Devon line, up trains

From	To	Loads (vehicles) Passenger or mixed traffic engine	Loads (vehicles) Goods Engine	Remarks
Torrington	Yeoford	50	50	Trains can take 60 wagons from Fremington to Barnstaple. Two wagons loaded with coal should be counted as three except between Fremington and Barnstaple. The load of the 12.55 pm from Torrington to be limited to 28 vehicles on arrival at Portsmouth Arms for crossing purposes.

North Cornwall and Bude lines, down trains

From	To	Loads (vehicles) Passenger or mixed traffic engine	Loads (vehicles) Goods Engine	Remarks
Meldon Junction	Halwill Junction	30	30	The 3.13 am from Okehampton to Wadebridge is limited to 25 vehicles Okehampton to Camelford and to 20 vehicles west of St Kew Highway.
Halwill Junction	Launceston	35	35	
Launceston	Egloskerry	30	30	
Egloskerry	Camelford	25	25	
Camelford	Padstow	35	35	
Halwill Junction	Dunsland Cross	35	35	
Dunsland Cross	Bude	30	30	

North Cornwall and Bude lines, up trains

From	To	Loads (vehicles) Passenger or mixed traffic engine	Loads (vehicles) Goods Engine	Remarks
Padstow	Wadebridge	30	30	The 4.25 pm train from Wadebridge to be limited to 20 wagons throughout. The 4.20 am from Holsworthy weekdays and the 4.5 am from Bude on Sundays should be limited to 20 vehicles. Three empty wagons to be counted as two loaded. Two heavily laden wagons, such as coal, sand etc, to be counted as three.
Wadebridge	Delabole	20	20	
Delabole	Otterham	25	25	
Otterham	Ashwater	35	35	
Ashwater	Halwill Junction	30	30	
Halwill Junction	Meldon Junction	35	35	
Bude	Holsworthy	25	25	
Holsworthy	Halwill Junction	35	35	

Chard Branch

Up and down trains 25

Seaton Branch

Up and down trains 25

From	To	Loads (vehicles) Passenger or mixed traffic engine	Loads (vehicles) Goods Engine	Remarks
Sidmouth Branch, down trains				
Sidmouth Junction	Tipton	45		
Tipton	Sidmouth Junction	16	Large Tank	
Tipton	Sidmouth Junction	16	Small Tank	
Sidmouth Branch, up trains				
Sidmouth	Tipton	Not stated		
Tipton	Sidmouth Junction	Not stated	Large Tank	
Tipton	Sidmouth Junction	Not stated	Small Tank	
Tipton and Exmouth Branch, down trains				
Tipton	East Budleigh	Not stated		
East Budleigh	Budleigh Salterton	16		
Budleigh Salterton	Exmouth	25		
Tipton and Exmouth Branch, up trains				
Exmouth	Budleigh Salterton	16		
Budleigh Salterton	Tipton	35		
Exmouth Branch, down trains				
Exeter	Exmouth	32		
Exmouth Branch, up trains				
Exmouth	Exeter	30		
Ilfracombe Branch, down trains				
Barnstaple	Braunton	50		
Braunton	Barnstaple	12	Large Tank	
Braunton	Barnstaple	11	Small Tank	

700 class 0-6-0 No 30315 stands on the up main line at Yeoford facing towards Exeter. Whilst the period is BR, the general scene would have been recognisable in the time of S. W. Milford, with the two starting signals respectively for the bay and main platforms. *S. W. C. Eyers collection*

Issued by Henry Holmes in 1910, the personal copy of S. W. Milford.

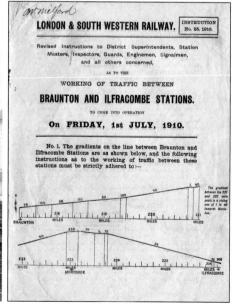

From	To	Loads (vehicles) Passenger or mixed traffic engine	Loads (vehicles) Goods Engine	Remarks
Ilfracombe Branch, up trains				
Ilfracombe	Mortehoe	12	Large Tank	
Ilfracombe	Mortehoe	11	Small Tank	
Mortehoe	Braunton	16		
Braunton	Barnstaple Junction	50		
Bodmin Branch, down trains				
Wadebridge	Boscarne Junction	–		
Boscarne Junction	Bodmin	–		
Bodmin Branch, up trains				
Bodmin	Boscarne Junction	21	With one van	
Bodmin	Boscarne Junction	25	With two vans	
Boscarne Junction	Wadebridge	30		
Wenford Mineral Branch, down trains				
Boscarne Junction	Wenford	25		
Wenford Mineral Branch, up trains				
Wenford	Boscarne Junction	20		
Cattlewater and Plymstock Branches				
Friary	Cattlewater	40		Three empty wagons count as two loaded except crocodile wagons one of which is to be counted as a loaded wagon.
Cattlewater	Friary	30		
Plymstock	Turnchapel	13		
Turnchapel	Plymstock	13		
Plymstock	Bayly's siding	11		
Bayly's siding	Plymstock	11		
Stonehouse Pool Branch, up and down trains				
		10		
Sutton Harbour Branch, up and down trains				
		9		
Laira Branch				
Friary	Laira	40		
Laira	Friary	30		

This is followed by an alphabetical index giving an insight into the statutory obligations of railways, and not surprisingly the LSWR in particular as well as examples of local services/facilities available. For example, under 'B' we have an entry, 'Bideford may supply vessels with water at 1/- each for any quantity not exceeding 250 gallons.' Then a useful aide-memoire: 'Bricks – 3,000 is the quantity to be loaded into an ordinary 10 ton truck.' We also find reference to the Block System and the undertaking given to the Board of Trade that the Block System will be used on all lines open 'for the conveyance of passengers'. This document is undated but would likely relate to Mr Milford's time in Hampshire as the example provided makes specific mention of one line only, that from Botley to Bishops Waltham, where such regulations would not apply provided only one engine is allowed upon the line at the same time.

Exactly when Mr Milford compiled this record is not certain but it may be reasonable to assume it referred to paperwork he collated during his career. As he rose in seniority he also included examples of documents that would only be the province of senior staff, such as the circumstances and conditions when an accident need be reported to the Board of Trade and also the requirements of the Board of Trade relative to the opening of new railways. So far as the former was concerned, we learn that a notice had to be seen 'within 24 hours' in the event of a fatal accident and 'as soon as practicable' in other cases. Numerous examples of notifiable accidents are given which are certainly not listed here but

When reproduced in the *Railway Magazine* for June 1911 (which issue included a lengthy feature on the London & South Western Railway), this view was captioned as a 'Special train of vans from Waterloo to Southampton'. More accurately it should be a '"K10" No 389 on fruit vans at Eastleigh, 31 January 1911' and thus very soon after Milford's appointment to the district. *NRM – Curl collection*

which include failures relative to locomotive power and rolling stock, ie boilers, wheels, tyres and axles, failures of permanent way and works etc, rail fractures, failures of bridges, tunnels, cuttings and embankments, or miscellaneous accidents such as train derailments, trains becoming divided, level crossing run-throughs, fires on trains, etc.

In the latter category (new railways and facilities) we are told, as an example, in paragraph 12 (1896 requirement) that, 'Platforms to be continuous and not less than 6 feet wide for stations of small traffic, nor less than 12 feet wide for important stations, the descents at the ends of the platforms to be by ramps and not by steps. Pillars, for the support of roofs and other fixed works, not to be less than 6 feet from the edges of the platforms. The height of the platforms above rail level to be 3 feet, save under exceptional circumstances, and in no case less than 2 feet 6 inches. The edges of the platforms to overhang not less than 12 inches. As little space as possible to be left between the edges of the platforms and those of the footboards on the carriages. Shelter to be provided on every platform and conveniences where necessary. Names of stations to be shown on boards and on the platform lamps.'

We know little else of his time at Exeter, although in 1905 there is a copy of a letter in the file to G. T. Vallance, the then Exeter Superintendent, from Dugald Drummond at Nine Elms, confirming that Milford (jnr) may be given the next available vacancy at Exmouth Junction depot. In what role, and likewise whether as a new entrant or a transferee, is not stated. Whilst this might at first glance appear to be nepotism, it should be recalled that at that time new entrants at least were usually taken from the families of existing staff in preference over rank outsiders. The subsequent career of Milford (jnr) is not referred to again.

Six years later on 1 January 1911 S. W. Milford moved upon promotion to the post of District Superintendent of the Central District at Eastleigh. This was confirmed in a letter of the same date, signed by Henry Holmes who occupied the role of Superintendent of the Line at Waterloo. Holmes refers to Milford's appointment as having been sanctioned by the LSWR directors, the role having with it a salary of £275 pa. (The average wage for a working man was then in the order of £60-£100 annually.)

We may also correctly assume that Mr Milford had been a popular man during his 30-plus years at Exeter – possibly because in one of the references we have to his role there we know that as chief clerk he had the responsibility of spending two days every week travelling around the District acting as pay clerk. As such he would have become known to most of the staff. This clearly held him in good stead, for at a presentation at Exeter to mark his departure, it was reported that no less a sum than £63 14s had been collected on his behalf.

Early in 1911 he was also approached by the embryonic *South Western Gazette* to feature in the magazine and he produced three typed pages of script. Whether anything was used, we cannot be certain, but his written text is almost totally related to naming men he had worked with and their subsequent career moves and, as such, sadly, has little interest today. One snippet relative to a specific name, though, is of interest and that is the mention of Mr Ellen, who in 1911 held the position of Superintendent at Southampton. One is immediately tempted to suggest then that Southampton was a separate District but we should recall the position to which he had been appointed, 'District Superintendent of the Central District', and it is therefore possible that the reference to Mr Ellen's position was what we later knew as Station Master, who in earlier times was referred to as 'Superintendent'.

It would be interesting to know exactly the boundaries of the Central District and therefore Milford's area of responsibility. Realistically this was probably bounded by

Salisbury and Dorchester in the west, Basingstoke in the north and likely Portsmouth in the east. As such he would have undoubtedly attended various incidents and occurrences and it is with reference to this that we may now refer to the only photographs that accompany his papers, which relate to the Andover Junction accident of 13 October 1914 but without any accompanying notes or report.

The aftermath of the Andover Junction accident, 13 October 1914. 'H15' No 488 at the head of a 40-wagon up market train has run into the rear of a stationary Yeovil to Nine Elms goods, scattering wagons and contents in its wake. D. L. Bradley provides a good description of this accident in Part 2 of the *Locomotives of the LSWR*, page 170, published by the RCTS, but without attributing a cause. Here was the scene once daylight had broken,

The aftermath of the Andover Junction accident, 13 October 1914. 'H15' No 488 at the head of a 40-wagon up market train has run into the rear of a stationary Yeovil to Nine Elms goods, scattering wagons and contents in its wake. D. L. Bradley provides a good description of this accident in Part 2 of the *Locomotives of the LSWR*, page 170, published by the RCTS, but without attributing a cause. Here was the scene once daylight had broken, with wagon debris all around and a crane attempting to make order out of chaos. Fortunately there were no human casualties, although with at least one laden livestock wagon involved it is unlikely that this was the case as far as the cattle were concerned. No 488 suffered minimal damage and, once re-railed, was able to be taken to Eastleigh works immediately. Besides giving the location, the rear of the image having the end view of the crane, he mentions that the figure seen in the hat and looking towards the camera is indeed S. W. Milford.

with wagon debris all around and a crane attempting to make order out of chaos. Fortunately there were no human casualties, although with at least one laden livestock wagon involved it is unlikely that this was the case as far as the cattle were concerned. No 488 suffered minimal damage and, once re-railed, was able to be taken to Eastleigh works immediately. Besides giving the location, the rear of the image having the end view of the crane, he mentions that the figure seen in the hat and looking towards the camera is indeed S. W. Milford.

There is now nothing until mention of his retirement on the date stated (31 December 1923) at the beginning of this article. Obviously we know he had at some stage moved to Southampton, presumably the District Superintendent post had been relocated, but again this is not certain. We do know that he had sat as a member of the Southampton Harbour Board and again had been a most popular manager whilst in

post. Indeed, the staff of the Central District arranged a retirement party and musical party for Mr and Mrs Milford on 14 January 1924, which was held in his honour at the Docks and Marine Sports Club Room, Southampton. The invitation was sent to his home address of 'Kinross', Grosvenor Road, Portswood, Southampton. His retirement details also featured in *Modern Transport* for 1924 but once again without elucidation. He also received several letters from colleagues and even officers of the Great Western Railway.

Clearly a private man, S. W. Milford was one of likely hundreds of whom we would now refer to as middle and senior managers whose career details have been all but lost. It would be wonderful to be able to add more to the story but nearly a century later the chances of this happening must be remote, unless of course a SW reader knows different ...?

The LSWR at Battledown just west of Basingstoke. Taken from a painting by F. Stafford and presented to the LSW Railwaymen's Institute at Vauxhall by Dugald Drummond.

From Stockbridge to Towcester

Roger Simmonds

Stockbridge station around the start of the 20th century. It would appear likely that both Stockbridge and Towcester may have suffered from ingress of damp at some stage, Stockbridge being slate hung and Towcester rendered. The similarities between the two may be noted, even down to the canopy roof lights. At a later stage the Stockbridge canopy lost its hip roof to be replaced by a straight provision.

A random and somewhat idle perusal through photographs can, from time to time, throw up some interesting similarities. Take station buildings, for example, where each original railway company who built a line might use a potential standard design according to the planned facilities to be provided and likely traffic needs, usually in accord with the size of the town or rural locations served. This is hardly surprising, particularly with larger companies like the London & South Western Railway (LSWR) or London, Brighton & South Coast Railway (LBSCR).

However, on occasions one can find strong similarities between unrelated lines geographically distant. Typically, smaller railway companies might utilise and adapt an 'off the shelf' design more often than not prepared by their appointed engineer or perhaps in some cases the contractor building the line. Unusual features can therefore stand out enough to draw reasonable comparisons.

One such possible case concerns Stockbridge station on the Andover & Redbridge line (later part of the LSWR) and Towcester station on the original Northampton & Banbury Junction Railway (later merged as the Stratford & Midland Junction Railway), neither having any known political or business connection with the other save perhaps the odd wagon or load destined from one system to the other. Certainly there was never any direct physical link between the two.

So why the connection? Well, simply through the two images. Coincidence perhaps but unlikely; a comparison of the two reveals an identical hipped central section to the canopy.

We are unaware of any other stations that had this distinctive feature and so we would certainly be glad to hear from any other SW readers if they know differently. What could be the link between these apparently unconnected companies? Both lines were constructed and opened in the 1860s and are therefore contemporary to the architectural tastes of the period.

Likely it is that the Engineer, John Collister, was engaged on both railways. He was certainly not averse to coming up with something unusual in station design as he demonstrated nearer to home with Bishops Waltham, where he was the Engineer to the Bishops Waltham company, again in a similar period, although Bishops Waltham was not in the same style. Collister had been an assisting engineer to Charles Vignoles before setting out on his own and was engaged by a number of railway companies in the UK and Ireland. (A trawl through the internet reveals Collister to have been involved in several railway schemes prior to his death in 1868.) Even so, there is no demonstrable evidence to say that Collister utilised drawings from Towcester and transplanted them to Stockbridge or vice versa, but it would seem likely.

Towcester from the camera of Edward Wallis. We may reasonably assume the original buildings of both were also identical on the approach side. Station facilities and other structures were different, however, as specified by the operating companies and local traffic needs.

Interlude
War Comes to Fullerton Junction

As a link between this item and the previous one, we need look no further than a few miles north of Stockbridge and the rural location of Fullerton Junction. Here was a station whose facilities certainly exceeded local needs but had come about in consequence of the connection between the Andover–Redbridge line running basically north-south and the southwest-northeast link from Fullerton to Hurstbourne. How any of this latter line was built was a matter of politics in the 19th century – basically an abortive attempt to keep the Didcot, Newbury & Southampton Railway (DNS) and therefore the Great Western Railway (GWR) away from Southampton. Further elaboration is not necessary for this piece but suffice to say this blocking line failed to secure its intended purpose – the GWR reaching Southampton via Winchester Chesil – and the little Hurstbourne to Fullerton route was a proverbial white elephant from the outset. Indeed, so much so that what had originally been laid out as a double-track railway was reduced to a single line as early as 1913 and then lost its passenger service in 1931, at the same time being severed at the Hurstbourne end to become in effect a long siding running from Fullerton.

Having set the scene, the remaining branch was for several years little more than a goods facility serving the intermediate stations of Wherwell and Longparish, the former yielding little traffic but there was a reasonable amount from what had become the terminus at Longparish where timber was handled from the adjacent Harewood

Forest. It is likely that, had World War 2 not intervened, the line would have been closed completely, probably as soon as some major engineering work or replacement became necessary. The 1940s, though, were to see an unexpected resurgence in two ways. Firstly at Longparish, where an ammunition storage depot was established, and then in 1940, when, due to attention from enemy bombing, much of the office accommodation previously associated with the operation of the docks was moved to a number of box vans and at least two coaches in one of the former Longparish line platforms at Fullerton station. A special train ran each morning and evening from Southampton to Fullerton and return at the start and end of each shift.

The normal passenger service between Fullerton and Hurstbourne in the final years was limited to a single coach, such was the paucity of traffic. Here Adams 0-4-2 No 614 awaits departure from Fullerton with an up train for Hurstbourne. The platform used during the 1940s as office accommodation was the one on the left. The buildings were situated in the 'V' of the junction between the two lines, with the Andover–Redbridge route running north-south (right to left) behind the structure.

Above: **Fullerton as recorded on 23 December 1940. The former London & South Western Railway coach is recorded as No 7841 – note the blackout paint around the windows. Each van – with modified door – served a different purpose and had separate telephone communication. The one that can be read is 'S M E Accounts'. It is not known how long the offices were based here.**

Strawberries and Steam

Richard Simmons

(Previous articles by Richard Simmons dealing with railway operation and featuring the Control Office at Southampton and later life at Wimbledon have appeared in *Southern Way* issues 6, 8, 12, 16, 28, 29 and 33.)

Fruit loading board at either Swanwick or Botley. Soft fruit had been grown in the area from early times. Indeed, before the days of foreign imports enabling soft fruit to be available throughout the year, Hampshire strawberries were always among the first of the season (an extreme example being in the mild winter of December 1818 when a crop was reported from Fareham). Until the early 1930s, strawberries were grown in the open and with the aid of glass cloches which helped to protect the ripening fruit. Polythene tunnels were introduced in the 1960s. The industry flourished in the early 20th century, although from the 1960s it began to decline. As many growers went out of business, much of the area previously covered by vast strawberry fields was developed for housing from the 1980s. Today there remain only a limited number, mainly of 'pick your own' facilities. *John Bailey*

We railway *aficionados* very likely thought we were doing well during the summer of 2016 with two BBC television series devoted to railway matters. The first, 'Trainspotting Live', seemed to be centred on just that – and the way it was presented conjured up quite an amount of criticism in various railway magazines. Far be it for me in this article to express my detailed thoughts of the series but suffice it to say I found it 'disappointing'. Meanwhile, the other series, 'Full Steam Ahead' concentrated on the impact on the country as a whole of the coming and spread of the nation's railway network. It highlighted, for example, the ease of movement rail conveyance provided for such perishable foodstuffs as fish from Whitby, rhubarb from Yorkshire and, in SW territory, watercress from Alresford.

Although the programmes concentrated on the carriage of these products from the producers' point of view, one omission was any insight from the railway operators regarding how they provided the resources to move such traffic, which peaked for a few weeks each year. It would be all too easy to sit and pick holes for the sake of it, but suffice to say there were a few omissions (practicalities included) and the series did not include strawberry traffic, especially that which originated from stations geographically not far from Alresford.

This article seeks to redress that imbalance and explain something of the organisation required to move this traffic during the limited season occurring from about late May/early June into July, covering part of the era when this traffic was rail conveyed. (Mention should also be made of other series on railways which have recently graced our screens, including, in the autumn of 2016, 'Railways: The Making of a Nation', plus the continuing travels of a certain Michael Portillo and more recently a new series, 'Extreme Railways', fronted by Chris Tarrant.)

Mention of strawberries is doubtless a reminder of the annual tournament on the hallowed tennis courts at Wimbledon, where thousands of punnets of fruit are consumed. Strawberry cultivation was once prominent over quite a large swathe of southern Hampshire but in more recent times much of the former growing areas have been covered by bricks and mortar or are under the tarmac and concrete of the M27 and other assorted road 'improvements'. Nevertheless, there were – and still seem to be – some growing towards the west of the county as, at least twice during the summer of 2016, local supermarkets have displayed strawberries bearing labels proclaiming they were Hampshire grown in the New Forest (also available were Scottish-grown strawberries from Angus). Now, with no disrespect whatsoever to the good people of Scotland, it might have been thought that the Scottish climate was too inhospitable to grow strawberries, although it is likely that they are all cultivated in the giant polythene tunnels so often seen in the countryside.

This article centres on south Hampshire-grown fruit conveyed by rail between 1950 and 1960. For those years our editor has been fortunate in procuring bound copies of the Southern (or Southampton) District special traffic arrangements (printed notices or 'P' notices) and I am greatly indebted to him for loaning me them to glean relevant details relating to strawberries.

The strawberry notices were produced annually and were joint ones covering both the Southern and London West Districts. Locally, the principal loading stations were at Botley, Bursledon and Swanwick and to a lesser extent Netley and Woolston. Mention must also be made of the former Meon Valley line station of Wickham. Officially traffic here ceased when the line closed in February 1955, although in fact it seemed to come to an end before closure, as will be seen as this article progresses. In west Hampshire, traffic emanated from both Lymington Pier and Lymington Town stations together with Brockenhurst on the main line.

Most strawberries were conveyed in vans either by special van trains or, when traffic was insufficient to form a complete van train, in vans attached to ordinary passenger services, which in those days were all steam-hauled, of course. Due to their perishable nature, it was only with minor exceptions that freight trains were used. Smaller consignments were carried in brake vans of individual services.

So to the notices, which, it will be seen, did not include starting or terminating dates or dates of running of individual services. This is simply explained by the vagaries of climate: a warm spell could bring forward the dates for picking, whilst cold would delay the time when the fruit was ready. In fact, it was a programme of services to be operated when necessary to meet traffic demands and notices included a short paragraph advising that operating dates of special workings would be announced by subsequent notices; most likely this would have been by means of daily stencil ('SN') notices, plus very short notice revisions by Trains Supervision Offices (Control). The period of validity of these notices would have been approximately mid- to late June through to late July/early August, again depending upon the vagaries of typical British summer weather. For the purpose of this article and especially when comparing the arrangements year by year, the 12-hour clock is used as this appears in the actual notices. Lest it be thought that empty van trains to loading stations have been excluded from the notices, none was included until about the end of the decade. Timings for such van workings would also have been published in daily SN notices when vehicle

Loading strawberries at Swanwick in London & South Western Railway days. Local folklore has it that the station here was provided specifically because of the strawberry traffic. For a short time each year it was one of the busiest in the country and extra-long platforms were built to load up the 'Strawberry Special' trains that departed regularly for Covent Garden market and other buyers across Britain. Small boys were employed for 3d (1¼p) an hour to load baskets on to the specially constructed shelves in the railway vans. By 1898, 7,000 tons of strawberries were being sent to London alone from this area. Many more were sold locally or sent to other locations in the UK. (As can be seen from the photograph, it was not just vans that were used for the traffic but also passenger-carrying vehicles.) This was the reason for employing boys, who, because of their diminutive stature, were able to reach into all corners and maximise the load that might be carried, often in vehicles hardly designed for the purpose. How they were unloaded at destination is another matter! Note also the procession of traders' carts and wagons on the station approach waiting to be dealt with. *Tony Sedgwick/Ian Wilkins*

Loading the train at Wickham in the summer of 1908. To the editor's inexpert eye, the vehicle on the left appears to be of London & North Western Railway origin. Working in the strawberry industry, the picking season was the most important and busiest time of the year, running from the end of May through to mid July. This was when local growers made the income which would pay their debts and keep their families for the rest of the year. Families, friends and neighbours were employed as pickers. Additional labour was supplied by gypsies and other casual workers. School children were also given 'picking holidays' to help with the work. The nearest similarity might be the hop-pickers' trains in Kent where living accommodation was also provided, it is not believed a similar provision was provided in Hampshire.

availability became known. Likewise, some destination station names have changed over the years, so contemporary names are used eg Manchester London Road and not the present name of Manchester Piccadilly. Meanwhile, some stations then open have since been closed. When vans were attached to ordinary services, times quoted are those operating during the summer timetable for the respective year. Should the season have started when the previous winter's timetable was in operation, any different timings for that period are not noted as they would have only applied for a relatively limited period.

Year by year, the notices commenced with a series of general instructions reminding loading stations that they must ensure that vans loaded to other Regions were, in all cases, suitable for working by express passenger services. When vehicles were loaded with mixed loads for transhipment, care had to be taken to ensure traffic for each destination was sorted and loaded separately to facilitate necessary reloading at other stations and distribution at point of transhipment.

Stations had to consult their District office before attaching any vehicles, in order that arrangements could be satisfactorily co-ordinated and waste haulage of lightly loaded vans obviated. Advices of all despatches had also to be made concurrent with their departures. London market traffic would include the consignee's details and weights and, in the case of transfer vans, the number of packages for each destination was given. Stations also had to maintain close liaison with Eastleigh Passenger Rolling Stock section in order to ensure maintenance of a satisfactory supply of vans.

It was essential that traffic was handled with care and by the services detailed in order to reduce to a minimum complaints and claims, which implies that they did indeed arise from time to time. Any matter of doubt concerning service, etc, had to be referred to District office for clarification. Finally, signal boxes had to be open to meet traffic requirements.

So much for the administration side of the operation; now for the 'nitty gritty' or the operation's front line year by year, where we find traffic was split into groups.

Starting in 1950, it appears that no special fruit notices were published for this year and, as notices were numbered consecutively throughout the year, there is no evidence in the bound volume that any are missing.

So to the first year for which we have full details: 1951. Destinations were grouped by letter with Group 'A' seemingly all London Midland Region (LMR) locations. Thus we find traffic sent via Andover Junction and the Midland & South Western Junction Railway (MSWJ) for Birmingham (New Street), Derby, Leeds, Nottingham (presumably Midland and not Victoria) and Bradford (Forster Square). In addition Group 'A' trains were routed via Willesden Junction for: Manchester (London Road), Liverpool (Lime Street), Burnley, Southport, Blackpool, Nelson, Colne, Blackburn, Accrington, Huddersfield and Carlisle. Note that trains via the MSWJ were for ex-Midland Railway stations and via Willesden to London & North Western (LNWR) and Lancashire & Yorkshire (L&Y) stations. Group 'A' vans via Willesden Junction to northern destinations had to be labelled as such. When traffic was light, a single vehicle or small

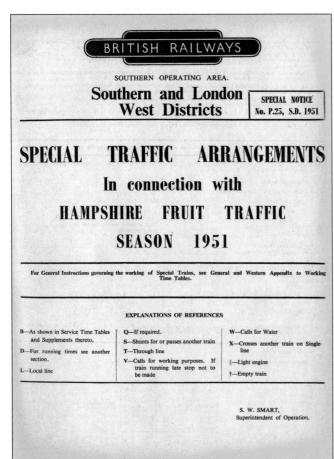

BRITISH RAILWAYS

SOUTHERN OPERATING AREA.

Southern and London West Districts

SPECIAL NOTICE
No. P.25, S.D. 1951

SPECIAL TRAFFIC ARRANGEMENTS
In connection with
HAMPSHIRE FRUIT TRAFFIC
SEASON 1951

For General Instructions governing the working of Special Trains, see General and Western Appendix to Working Time Tables.

EXPLANATIONS OF REFERENCES

B—As shown in Service Time Tables and Supplements thereto.

D—For running times see another section.

L—Local line

Q—If required.

S—Shunts for or passes another train

T—Through line

V—Calls for working purposes. If train running late stop not to be made

W—Calls for Water

X—Crosses another train on Single line

‖—Light engine

†—Empty train

S. W. SMART,
Superintendent of Operation.

2

No. 1—Stations loading vans must ensure that those loaded to other Regions are, in all cases, suitable for working by express passenger services.

Where vehicles are loaded with mixed loads for transhipment, care must be taken to ensure that traffic for each destination is sorted and loaded separately in order to facilitate loading at other stations and distribution upon arrival at point of transhipment.

Stations must consult their District Office before arranging to attach any vehicles, in order that arrangements may be satisfactorily co-ordinated and waste haulage by lightly-loaded vans obviated.

Advices of all despatches must be advised currently. Traffic to London Markets must include details of consignees and weights, and in the case of transfer vans the number of packages for each destination must be given.

Stations must maintain close liaison with the Passenger Rolling Stock Section, Eastleigh (Telephone 900 or 954), in order to ensure the maintenance of a satisfactory supply of vans.

It is essential that the traffic is handled with care and by the services detailed in order to reduce to a minimum complaints and claims.

Any matters of doubt concerning service, etc., should be referred to District Office for clarification.

No. 2—OPENING OF SIGNAL BOXES.—Signal boxes to be open to meet the requirements of the traffic.

GROUP 'A' TRAFFIC (via ANDOVER JUNCTION) FOR BIRMINGHAM (NEW STREET), DERBY, LEEDS, NOTTINGHAM AND BRADFORD (FOSTER SQUARE)

When traffic is light

No. 3—From Netley Line Stations and Botley

Vans to be despatched by 1.28 p.m. ex Romsey, to work as under:—

	p.m.	p.m.	
Fareham	2 32	3 12	A—To Cheltenham
Botley	3 21½	3 23	
Eastleigh	3 34	4 22	Vans to be labelled via Andover Junction
Romsey	4 37	4 54	and Cheltenham
Andover Junction	5 34	5A38	

No. 4—Traffic from Wickham

To be forwarded by 2.13 p.m. to Fareham, thence by service shown above.

No. 5—From Lymington and Brockenhurst

Vans to work as under:—

	SX		SO	
	p.m.	p.m.	a.m.	a.m.
Lymington Pier		1 22		10 35
Lymington Town	1 24	1 25	10 37	10 39
Brockenhurst	1 36	1 56	10 49	1 5
Eastleigh	2 31	4 22	1 55	4 22
Romsey	4 37	4 54	4 37	4 54
Andover Junction	5 34	5A38	5 34	5A38

When insufficient traffic is available for individual through vans loads, it must (if of sufficient volume) be loaded into a vehicle labelled 'Birmingham Transfer' and full details of traffic loaded into this van must be advised by each loading Station.

When traffic is heavy

From Netley Line Stations and Botley

Special Train—(If required)

No. 6

	arr. p.m.	dep. p.m.	
Bursledon		2 45	C—Eastleigh to forward vans as shown in Service 3.
Swanwick	2 50	3 18	
Fareham	3 26	3 35	
Botley	3 46	3 58	
Eastleigh	4 10	C	

3

No. 7—From Lymington and Brockenhurst

As shown in Service 5.

No. 8—Traffic from Wickham to be forwarded by 2.13 p.m. Fareham to marshal vans into 3.35 p.m. special thence.

GROUP 'A' TRAFFIC (via WILLESDEN) FOR MANCHESTER (LONDON ROAD), LIVERPOOL (LIME STREET), BURNLEY, SOUTHPORT, BLACKPOOL, NELSON, COLNE, BLACKBURN, ACCRINGTON, HUDDERSFIELD AND CARLISLE

WHEN TRAFFIC IS LIGHT THE FOLLOWING SERVICES WILL APPLY:—

No. 9—From Netley Line Stations and Botley

Vans to be despatched by 1.28 p.m. ex Romsey, thence as under (Passenger vans must be utilised):—

	p.m.	p.m.	
Fareham	2 32	3 12	Vans to be labelled via Willesden
Botley	3 21½	3 23	
Eastleigh	3A34	3 42	A—Eastleigh to detach vans labelled via Andover Junction.
Basingstoke	4 31	5 37	C—to Kensington Sidings.
Waterloo	7 8	7 25	
Clapham Junction	7C40	8 10	
Willesden	8 30		

Special Train

No. 10

	arr. p.m.	dep. p.m.
Waterloo	(7 8)	7 25L
Queens Road		7 33T
Clapham Jct.		7C40

No. 11—Traffic from Wickham

To be forwarded by 2.13 p.m. to Fareham, thence by service shown above.

No. 12—From Lymington and Brockenhurst

Vans to work as under:—

	SX		SO	
	p.m.	p.m.	a.m.	a.m.
Lymington Pier		1 22		10 35
Lymington Town	1 24	1 25	10 37	10 39
Brockenhurst	1 36	1 56	10 49	1 5
Eastleigh	2 31		1 55	C

C—Thence as shown above.

No. 13

	Altered 2.45 p.m. Portsmouth and Southsea	
	arr. p.m.	dep. p.m.
Eastleigh	3B34	3 42
Shawford	3 49	3 50
Winchester City	3 57	3 59
Winchester Junction		4 41
Micheldever	4 14	4 15
Worting Jct.		4 27L
Basingstoke	4 31	4B45

4

WHEN TRAFFIC IS HEAVY, THE FOLLOWING WORKING WILL APPLY—

FOR DESTINATIONS IN GROUP 'A' (via Willesden) AND GROUP 'C'.

SPECIAL TRAIN (if required)

No. 14

	arr. p.m.	dep. p.m.
Bursledon		1 55
Swanwick	2 0	2 38
Fareham	2E46	
Fareham		3 18
Botley	3 30	3 40
Eastleigh	3F50	3 55
Winchester Jct.		4 10
Worting Jct.		4 33T
Basingstoke	4 38	4L43
Farnborough	T	
Woking		5 17
Hampton Court Jct.		5 31
Wimbledon A Box		5 40
East Putney		5 48
Pt. Pleasant Jct.		5 50L
Clapham Jct.	5 54	5 55
Latchmere Jct.		5 57
Kensington (O)	6 5	6 6
Willesden	6 17	

No. 15

'Q'

	arr. p.m.	dep. p.m.
Fratton	A	12 35
Portcreek Jct.		12 40
Cosham		12 44
Fareham	12 55	12 58
Bursledon	1 10	(1 55) (2 45)

Bursledon to provide brake van.

A—Will be one or two engines coupled as required.

E—Fareham to attach vans received ex Wickham.

F—Eastleigh to attach vans received ex Brockenhurst.

No. 16—Formation from Fareham to be Engine, Vans Glasgow and Edinburgh, Vans in Group 'A' via Willesden, Brake Van.

No. 17—From Lymington and Brockenhurst

Vans to work as under:—

	SX		SO	
	p.m.	p.m.	a.m.	a.m.
Lymington Pier		1 22		10 35
Lymington Town	1 24	1 25	10 37	10 39
Brockenhurst	1 36	1 56	10 49	1 5
Eastleigh	2 31	G	1 55	G

G—Thence as shown in service No. 14.

No. 18—Traffic from Wickham

To be forwarded to Fareham by 2.13 p.m.

Fareham to marshal vans into 3.18 p.m., special thence

No. 19—7.45 p.m. vans, Victoria to Kensington, diverted via Clapham Junction, as under:—

No. 20

	arr. p.m.	dep. p.m.	
Victoria		7B45	
	D	N	
Longhedge Junction		7 52	
Clapham Jct.	7A57	8 10	
Latchmere Junction		8 12	
Kensington (O)	8 20	8 21	
Willesden	8 30		

'A'—Attach vans received off 7.25 p.m. Waterloo.

5

GROUP 'B'—TRAFFIC FOR BRISTOL AND SOUTH WALES

Traffic will work as under:—

WHEN TRAFFIC IS LIGHT

No. 21—Traffic from Netley line Stations. From Swanwick and Bursledon ONLY by 4.35 p.m. ex Portsmouth and Southsea, for transfer at **Salisbury** into appropriate parcels vans on 5.35 p.m. Portsmouth and Southsea to Cardiff. (Other Netley line Stations and Fareham will load direct into the appropriate vans.)

No. 22—Traffic from Botley by 3.35 p.m. ex Portsmouth and Southsea for transfer at **Romsey** into appropriate parcels vans on 5.35 p.m. ex Portsmouth and Southsea.

No 23—Traffic from **Lymington and Brockenhurst** by 4.21 p.m. ex Lymington Town (4.18 p.m. Lymington Pier, commencing 18th June), for transfer at **Brockenhurst** into 4.38 p.m. ex Bournemouth Central and at **Southampton Central** into appropriate Parcels vans on 5.35 p.m. ex Portsmouth and Southsea to Cardiff.

No. 24—Traffic from **Wickham** to be forwarded by 2.13 p.m. to Fareham, thence as shown in Service No. 21.

WHEN TRAFFIC IS HEAVY

No. 25—Traffic from **Botley**. Small lots to be loaded into train van of 3.38 p.m. ex Portsmouth and Southsea for transfer at **Romsey** into the appropriate fruit van on the 4.0 p.m. special ex Fareham or 5.35 p.m. ex Portsmouth and Southsea, as the case may be.
Van loads to be despatched by the same services.

No. 26—Traffic from **Lymington and Brockenhurst** will work as shewn above, but transferred at **Southampton Central** into the appropriate fruit vans on the 4.0 p.m. special ex Fareham or 5.35 p.m. ex Portsmouth and Southsea, as the case may be.

No. 27—Traffic from **Wickham** to be forwarded by 2.13 p.m. to Fareham, thence by 4.0 p.m. special train.

Traffic from Netley Line Stations. A special train will be run as under (Saturdays excepted) when required:—

No. 28	arr. p.m.	dep. p.m.
Fareham		4 0
Swanwick	4 7	4 45
Bursledon	4 49	5 32
Netley	5 37	5F55
Woolston	6 1	6 15
St. Denys		6 21
Northam Jct.		6 23
Southampton Central	6T26	6 47
Redbridge		6 53
Romsey	7 6	7 22
Kimbridge Jct.		7 27
Alderbury Jct.		7 41
Tunnel Jct.		7 49½
Salisbury	7 53	8 6

Engine No. 29	arr. p.m.	dep. p.m.
Eastleigh South		2 50
Fareham	3 15	(4 0)

F—Train will run from Netley to Westbury when there are four or more vans.

On occasions when train is **not** extended to Westbury, vans will be attached at Netley to 5.35 p.m. Portsmouth and Southsea to Cardiff.
The train leaving Fareham to be formed of engine, loaded vans (if any), and Van 'C'.
The formation leaving **Swanwick** to be as under:—
Engine
Van (s) for South Wales stations other than Cardiff
Van (s) for Cardiff and/or Cardiff Transfer
Van (s) Bristol
Guard's van.
Any vans attached en route must be carefully marshalled.
On the occasions when this special train runs the normal Bristol van will **not** be provided from **Portsmouth and Southsea** by the 5.35 p.m.
Should the Bristol van provided on the Special train load heavily with fruit an additional van for this station must be provided from **Bursledon** at extreme rear (in order to replace the normal parcels vehicle). On such occasions, when special is extended to Westbury, **stations from Netley thence to load parcel traffic into Bristol van on this train instead of 5.35 p.m. ex Portsmouth and Southsea.**

6

GROUP 'C' TRAFFIC FOR EDINBURGH, ABERDEEN AND GLASGOW (St. Enoch)
GROUP 'F' TRAFFIC FOR NEWCASTLE, HULL AND MIDDLESBROUGH

Traffic in van loads will work as under:—

No. 30—**From Netley Line**
Will be despatched by 8.54 a.m. ex Romsey

No. 31—**From Wickham**
Will be despatched by 9.48 a.m. to Fareham

No. 32—**From Lymington Pier**
Will be despatched by 11.25 a.m.
Vehicles from all areas working as under:—

	arr.	dep.		arr.	dep.
Fareham	10 6 a.m.	11 17 a.m.	Brockenhurst	11 39 a.m.	11 55 a.m.
Botley	11 28 a.m.	11 29 a.m.	Eastleigh	12 31 p.m.	12H33 p.m.
Eastleigh	11 39 a.m.	12H33 p.m.			
	p.m.	p.m.			
Basingstoke	1 13	1H16			
Waterloo	2 19	2 25			
Clapham Jct.	2c38	3 23 to King's Cross.			
		3 30 to Willesden (See Service No. 35).			

Special Train 33

	arr. p.m.	dep. p.m.
Waterloo	(2 19)	2 25L
Queens Road		2¾34T
Clapham Jct.	2C38	

C—To Kensington Sidings
H—At extreme rear

When this train runs the following alteration will apply:—
2.30 p.m. Waterloo (W) to Teddington—Run on Local line from Queens Road.

If the load of 11.2 a.m. Bournemouth West exceeds platform acceptance at Waterloo, fruit vans to be detached at **Basingstoke** and work special thence as under:—

34 If Required		arr. p.m.	dep. p.m.
Basingstoke	A		1T34
Woking Jct.		2 5	
Hampton Court Jct.		2 17	
Wimbledon A. Box		2 26	
East Putney		2 32	
Pt. Pleasant Jct.		2 34L	
Clapham Jct.		2 36	D

A—With traffic detached from 11.2 a.m. Bournemouth West.

D—Vans, except Glasgow, connect with 3.23 p.m. E.R. trip to King's Cross. Vans for Glasgow (St. Enoch) connect with 3.30 p.m. trip to Willesden.

If this train runs the following train alterations will apply:—
2.13½ p.m. Teddington to Waterloo } Run on Through line from Barnes
2.14½ p.m. Hounslow to Waterloo }
12Q48 p.m. Southampton Docks to Waterloo—Revised to pass Woking Junction 2T/8 p.m. Hampton Court Junction 2/20 p.m., Clapham Junction 2/31 p.m. and arrive Waterloo 2.38 p.m.

Vans with traffic for Glasgow to go forward from Clapham Jct. by special train as under:—

35	arr. p.m.	dep. p.m.
Clapham Jct.		3 30
Latchmere Jct.		3 32
Kensington (O)	3 40	E

E—Traffic to go forward by 3.56 p.m. parcels train to Willesden.

7

No. 36—When vans for Glasgow (St. Enoch) are forwarded by the 11.2 a.m. ex Bournemouth West, the District Traffic Supt's. Office, Southampton to advise the District Traffic Superintendent's Office, Woking, (Extension 32) not later than 12.30 p.m. in order that arrangements can be made for the 2.0 p.m. ex Willesden to be extended to Clapham Jct.

No. 37—It is essential that vehicles utilised for these services are in Gauge to pass via the L.T.E. widened lines vide instructions shewn on page 170 of the coaching arrangements book, whilst they must be suitable for express passenger train working. These services are **not** available for Saturday despatches.
These services are **not** applicable to small lots of traffic, for which despatch details are shewn in a later paragraph.

No. 38—When 1.55 p.m. Bursledon to Willesden (Service) runs, vans from Netley Line Stations and Botley for Glasgow and Edinburgh must be marshalled with Glasgow vans (next engine) and Edinburgh vans next behind **arriving Willesden.** This matter to be given special attention.

GROUP 'D'—TRAFFIC FOR LONDON MARKETS (EXCEPT BRENTFORD)
GROUP 'E'—TRAFFIC FOR KEW BRIDGE (FOR BRENTFORD MARKET)

WHEN TRAFFIC LIGHT

No. 39—A van will be attached at Southampton Terminus to the rear of the 5.15 p.m., with a further van attached at Swanwick, if required. **Southampton Central** to return next engine 6.27 p.m. thence. The vehicle(s) to be transferred at Fareham to the 8.3 p.m. ex Portsmouth and Southsea, and at **Eastleigh** to the 6.30 p.m. Weymouth to Waterloo.

WHEN TRAFFIC HEAVY

Special train will run as under (Saturdays excepted):—

No. 40	arr. p.m.	dep. p.m.
Bevois Park		6†14
St. Denys		6 16
Woolston	6†21	6 30
Netley	6 36	6 46
Bursledon	6 51	7 25
Swanwick	7 30	8 5
Fareham	8 12	
Fareham		8 38
Botley	8 50	9 5
Eastleigh	9 15	

Engine for Service to run from Eastleigh to Bevois Park coupled with normal 4¾43 p.m.

The Formation of the train leaving Bevois Park will be:—
Engine
Van Kew Bridge
Brake van
Van Waterloo (or Nine Elms)

Attachments for these destinations will be made as required en route, but the marshalling shewn **must** be maintained and the running of the train given special attention in order to ensure its punctual arrival at **Eastleigh.**
Traffic to be forwarded from Eastleigh by the 10.15 p.m. (7.55 p.m. Bournemouth West vans) which is to be marshalled as under upon departure from the former station:—
Engine
Vans Waterloo or Nine Elms (Fruit Traffic)
Brake van
Vans Waterloo (Other than Fruit)
Vans Clapham Junction
Vans Kew Bridge
Vans Woking
Vans Reading
Engine to work this train forward from Eastleigh to be 'off' Eastleigh Motive Power Depot not later than 9.30 p.m., Motive Power Department to arrange.
The working of this train must be given special attention throughout in order to ensure its punctual arrival at Waterloo and delivery of fruit to morning markets.

No. 41—The traffic for London Markets (other than Brentford) will be dealt with at Waterloo up to a total of 4,000 Baskets but when in excess of this number will be handled at Nine Elms. Contact should, therefore, be maintained with this office in order that correct labelling can be carried out.

8

When traffic for London Markets is required to be dealt with at Nine Elms, the 7.55 p.m. van train from Bournemouth West, will be revised as under:—

	42 arr. a.m.	42 dep. a.m.	43 arr. a.m.	43 dep. a.m.
Clapham Jct.	12YB36	12TA40		12T48
Loco Jct.	12 45	12 47		
Nine Elms Shed	12 56			
Waterloo			12 56	

A—With vans for Nine Elms detached from 7.55 p.m. van train.

No. 44—Vans with traffic for Kew Bridge will be detached at Clapham Junction and forwarded by the 5.Q0 a.m. service, which train will run as required.
In the event of the traffic going through to Waterloo, it will be transferred to the 4.25 a.m. van train.

No. 45—On Sundays only, this traffic to be specially run from Clapham Junction to Kew Bridge in the following timing:—

Sunday when required	arr. a.m.	dep. a.m.
Clapham Jct.	A	4L15
Barnes		4¾21
Kew Bridge	4 30	

A—Control, Woking to advise all concerned when train is required to run.

No. 46—Traffic from Lymington and Brockenhurst will, in all cases, be despatched from Lymington Pier by the 7.46 p.m. (until 16th June; 7.27 p.m. from 18th June) to Brockenhurst and connect thence with 6.30 p.m. Weymouth to Waterloo (No traffic from these points will be sent to Nine Elms).

No. 47—Traffic from Wickham will work through as under

	p.m.	p.m.
Wickham		8 55
Alton	9 40	10 5
Woking	10 53	12 7 a.m.
Waterloo	12 48 a.m.	

No. 48—The following Freight Train revisions will apply on the occasions when the 6.14 p.m. special, Bevois Park to Eastleigh runs:—
6.10 p.m. Fareham to Netley .. : Start 6.45 p.m. and run to 'Q' timing.
6.44 p.m. Netley to Fareham .. : Start 7.30 p.m. and run to 'Q' timing.
7.55 p.m. Fareham to Eastleigh .. : Start 8.58 p.m. and run eight minutes later than the 'Q' Timing shewn in Freight Working Time Table.
The dates on which the special workings will operate will be advised by subsequent notices.

No. 49—Small consignments of Fruit destinations in Groups 'A', 'C' and 'F' will be despatched as under:—
From Netley Line and Botley Area by the 12.24 p.m. ex Southampton Central for transfer at Fareham into the 12.56 p.m. ex Portsmouth and Southsea, and at **Eastleigh** into the 1.5 p.m. Bournemouth West to Waterloo.
From Lymington and Brockenhurst by the 1.22 p.m. ex Lymington Pier for transfer at Brockenhurst into 1.5 p.m. Bournemouth West to Waterloo.

W. H. SCUTT,
District Traffic Superintendent
Southampton Central Station
31st May, 1951

(B 25 48043)

P. A. WHITE,
District Traffic Superintendent
Woking Station.

Hobbs the Printers Limited, 16-22 Shirley Road, Southampton

consignments would use the following services from Netley line stations (Woolston, Netley, Bursledon and Swanwick): 1.28pm Romsey–Portsmouth & Southsea as far as Fareham, thence by the 2.45pm Portsmouth & Southsea–Reading General which then also picked up at Botley, detaching any vans labelled via Andover Junction at Eastleigh. Otherwise fruit remained on the 2.45pm train as far as Basingstoke where it was transferred to the 5.37pm (4.3pm ex-Salisbury) to Waterloo. There it was loaded into a special van train, 7.25pm Waterloo–Clapham Junction (Kensington Sidings), where vans were attached to the 7.45pm Victoria–Willesden Junction vans, which was diverted via Clapham Junction, calling there from 7.57pm to 8.10pm. Traffic from Wickham (Meon Valley) left there at 2.13pm having been loaded on to the 1.30pm Alton–Fareham and similarly transferred at the latter station to the 2.45pm ex-Portsmouth & Southsea. Saturdays excepted, traffic from Lymington Pier and Lymington Town circulated on the 1.22pm Lymington Pier–Brockenhurst, loading also at Brockenhurst on to the 1.56pm Brockenhurst (1.5pm ex-Bournemouth West) as far as Eastleigh and again on to the 2.45pm ex-Portsmouth & Southsea). On Saturdays the 10.35 Lymington Pier–Brockenhurst was used, 1.5pm Brockenhurst (11.45 ex-Bournemouth West) to Eastleigh and on the 2.45pm ex-Portsmouth & Southsea.

During times of heavy traffic, a special van train started from Bursledon at 1.55pm to Willesden Junction, picking up at Swanwick, Fareham (reverse and attach vans from Wickham which had arrived at Fareham off the 1.30pm Alton–Fareham), Botley and Eastleigh, where vans from the Lymington branch and Brockenhurst were attached, having utilised the same services when traffic was light. This special van train then continued its journey via Basingstoke, Wimbledon, East Putney, Clapham Junction and Kensington Olympia, due at Willesden Junction 6.17pm. For this working a light engine pathway is shown leaving Fratton MPD at 12.35pm to Bursledon, the vans having previously been delivered to the station ready for loading.

Group 'B' was classified as being destined for Bristol and South Wales. When traffic was light from the Netley line stations of Swanwick and Bursledon, strawberries were loaded on to the 4.45pm Portsmouth & Southsea–Salisbury for transfer at Salisbury into what was described as 'appropriate parcel vans' on the 5.37pm Portsmouth & Southsea–Cardiff General. Fareham and other Netley line stations loaded their traffic directly into the same appropriate vans on the 5.37 ex-Portsmouth & Southsea, but which did not call at Swanwick and Bursledon, hence the earlier arrangement. Ex-Wickham traffic was again loaded into the 1.30pm Alton–Fareham for transfer at Fareham into the 5.37 ex-Portsmouth & Southsea. Meanwhile Botley traffic was loaded into the 3.35pm Portsmouth & Southsea–Romsey via Eastleigh, being transferred at Romsey into the same 5.37 ex-Portsmouth & Southsea. Produce from the Lymington branch used the 4.21pm Lymington Town–Brockenhurst; this train did not run from Lymington Pier (depart 4.18pm) until the commencement of the summer timetable on 18 June. How traffic from Lymington Pier was dealt with before

that date is unspecified; presumably the growers had to make their own arrangements as far as Lymington Town. Upon arrival at Brockenhurst, produce was transferred into the 4.38pm Bournemouth Central–Eastleigh but only as far as Southampton Central, where it too was transferred into the appropriate vans on the 5.37pm ex-Portsmouth & Southsea.

At peak times the Netley line was served by a special train, 4.0pm SX Fareham–Westbury, picking up at Swanwick, Bursledon, Netley, Woolston (which appears not to have warranted any special arrangements before), Southampton Central and Romsey. For this working an engine ran light from Eastleigh to Fareham. Interestingly, the formation was specified from Swanwick and not Fareham viz – engine, van(s) for South Wales other than Cardiff, van(s) for Cardiff and/or Cardiff transfer, van(s) Bristol and guard's van. Traffic from Botley defined as 'small lots' was loaded into the train van of the 3.38pm Portsmouth & Southsea–Romsey being transferred there into appropriate vans on the 5.37 ex-Portsmouth & Southsea. As usual, traffic from Wickham was forwarded on the 2.13pm (1.30pm ex-Alton), being transferred at Fareham into the 4.0pm van train when running. (Not geographically far from Wickham was the market town of Bishops Waltham and where again there was some strawberry growing. Bishops Waltham still had a railway at this time, although it was limited to goods operating just two or three times weekly, passenger services having been withdrawn many decades earlier. It is unlikely the irregular goods workings on the branch would have suited the growers in the area who instead would probably have taken their produce direct to the railhead at Botley, three miles distant.)

Group 'C' was traffic for the Scottish Region and the North East of England. This commenced its journey mid-morning with that from Netley line stations, starting on the 8.54am Romsey–Portsmouth & Southsea as far as Fareham, where it was transferred as far as Eastleigh on the 10.45am Portsmouth & Southsea–Winchester City, picking up en route at Botley. From here on life became somewhat complicated, because at Eastleigh vans were attached to the 11.2am Bournemouth West–Waterloo, which had already gained traffic from the Lymington branch at Brockenhurst off the 11.25 Lymington Pier–Brockenhurst. Upon arrival at Waterloo at 2.19pm, a quick detachment of vans (which were all on the rear) was made and an engine attached to form the 2.25pm van special to Clapham Junction (Kensington Sidings). A complication arose, however, if the total length of the 11.2am ex-Bournemouth West from Eastleigh exceeded the platform acceptance at Waterloo. Should this situation arise the vans had to be detached at Basingstoke to form a special van train (if required) running from Basingstoke–Clapham Junction via East Putney. Presumably a train crew and engine were rostered for this special, which would have been arranged following receipt of the train length by Southampton and the Woking Trains Supervision offices. By whichever means these services reached Clapham Junction, the Glasgow vans tripped forward the short distance to Kensington Olympia by a special van train leaving Clapham Junction at 3.30pm, connecting there with the 3.56pm parcels train thence to Willesden Junction.

An Eastern Region (hence the 'E' suffix to the running number) fruit van at Guildford on 27 March 1950. Whether such vehicles were worked down empty for trains in 'Group A' is not known. The type of vehicle seen here will also be noted to have a degree of ventilation. *S. W. C. Eyers collection*

When it is considered that none of these trains was of refrigerated vans and in the 21st century the shelf life of unrefrigerated strawberries is stated to be just a single day, it is remarkable how well the service operated. Equally, how did we all survive in those times eating food that had probably been in-transit for at least 24 hours?!

Group D was the London markets traffic excepting that destined for Brentford and Kew Bridge (for Brentford market). During periods of light traffic, a van followed a curious circuit, first finding itself on the rear of the 5.15pm Southampton Terminus–Southampton Central which, after reversal at Southampton Central, formed the 6.27pm Southampton Central–Portsmouth & Southsea, thus finding itself on the front leaving Southampton Central. But the 6.27pm ran via Southampton Terminus, where it reversed, so upon leaving that station lo and behold the van was on the rear again! If required, a further van was attached behind it at Swanwick. The van(s) were transferred at Fareham (depart 8.28pm) to the 8.3pm Portsmouth & Southsea–Eastleigh and at Eastleigh to the 6.30pm Weymouth–Waterloo (depart Eastleigh 9.7pm). When traffic was heavy, a special van train, Saturdays excepted, started from Woolston at 6.30pm, for which an engine ran light from Eastleigh to Bevois Park Sidings, where it attached empty vans, running empty at 6.14pm to Woolston thence as a loaded train to Eastleigh via Fareham (reverse). Formation of this train from Bevois Park Sidings was: engine, vans for Kew Bridge, brake van, van(s) for Waterloo or Nine Elms. The aforementioned marshalling had to be maintained and special attention given to its running to ensure punctual arrival at Eastleigh, from where vans were attached to the 7.55pm Bournemouth West–Waterloo vans, leaving Eastleigh at 10.15pm. Marshalling upon departure from Eastleigh was as follows: engine, vans for Waterloo or Nine Elms (the Nine Elms reference is fruit traffic destined for Nine Elms goods), brake van, vans for Waterloo (other than fruit), vans for Clapham Junction, vans for Kew Bridge, vans for Woking and finally vans for Reading. The motive power department was charged to arrange for the engine working this train forward from Eastleigh

to be 'off' Eastleigh MPD not later than 9.30pm, and the train's running had to be given special attention throughout to ensure punctual arrival at Waterloo at 12.48am, so as to ensure delivery of fruit to the morning markets.

Other than Brentford and Kew Bridge, traffic for London markets was dealt with at Waterloo, up to a maximum of 4,000 baskets, but the notice does not stipulate who had to count them because it continues by stating that when the number exceeded this figure it would be handled at Nine Elms. When this situation arose, the 7.55pm ex-Bournemouth West vans would divide at Clapham Junction with the front portion going to Nine Elms and the rear to Waterloo.

Traffic from the Lymington branch and Brockenhurst was despatched by the 7.27pm (summer timetable), 7.46pm (winter timetable), Lymington Pier–Brockenhurst connecting there into the 6.30pm Weymouth–Waterloo but no traffic from these stations was to go to Nine Elms. Meanwhile traffic from Wickham to London markets circulated via Alton on the 8.55pm from Wickham (8.43pm Fareham–Alton), transferring at Alton into unspecified services to Waterloo where arrival was at 12.48am, ie the 7.55pm ex-Bournemouth West–Waterloo vans, which by deduction means the fruit would have been transferred and reloaded at Woking.

The year 1951 will also be remembered for the Festival of Britain and notwithstanding the razzamatazz of festival events it was designed to show how good conditions in Great Britain now were following the end of World War 2 some six years earlier. But this glitz and glamour was in many ways superficial as several food stuffs remained on ration until July 1954. For the railways, too, it was not all good news, notwithstanding the various standard locomotives and types of rolling stock beginning to appear. Two weeks of the summer timetable, which should have finished on 23 September 1951, were lopped off; consequently the winter timetable started two weeks earlier than it should have done. Whilst the author is open to correction, I think the cause was either a fuel shortage or problems with national and international payments.

Group E traffic was for Kew Bridge, the railhead for Brentford Market. Vans for Kew Bridge reached London on the 7.55pm vans ex-Bournemouth West which, as has already been explained, at times of heavy traffic divided at Clapham Junction for Nine Elms and Waterloo. When the train divided at Clapham Junction, the Kew Bridge vans were also detached, going forward to Kew Bridge on a 5.0am 'Q' service from Clapham Junction. On Sunday mornings it was on a 4.15am special Clapham Junction to Kew Bridge as arranged by Woking Trains Supervision Office. When the Bournemouth train did not divide, the vans were worked to Kew Bridge on the 4.25am ex-Waterloo van train.

Many services already detailed were repeated each year, so the remainder of this article will be confined to year by year major alterations only.

Noteworthy in 1952 was that no traffic was shown as originating from Wickham, probably because by then the passenger service over the Meon Valley line had been reduced from five to four trains on weekdays, one such casualty being withdrawal of the 8.43pm Fareham–Alton. No doubt the cynics of the time contended that this was a precursor to total withdrawal of the passenger service, which did indeed come about in February 1955. Presumably fruit growers who had used Wickham had to arrange to take their produce to other stations, the nearest being either Fareham or Botley.

One feature of the 1952 notices was that more light engine timings were included than in the corresponding 1951 notice. Another feature was inclusion of arrangements for Kent-grown fruit to dovetail into arrangements for that grown in Hampshire. This related to vans on the 11.15am Ramsgate–Victoria via Chatham for the LMR via Willesden Junction and the Eastern Region (ER) via Kings Cross destinations. This train was due to arrive at Victoria at 2.10pm and, if required, a 2.32pm Victoria to Clapham Junction via Longhedge Junction trip operated, shown to be SR-worked. Upon arrival at Clapham Junction, ER destination vans were transferred to the 3.23pm to King's Cross and those for the LMR to the 3.30pm Victoria-Willesden Junction vans which was revised to start from Clapham Junction. To balance this, the 2.00pm Willesden Junction-Victoria vans was diverted from Latchmere Junction to terminate at Clapham Junction. Both trains were 'Q' workings and shown to be worked by the LMR.

In 1953 it was stated that when group 'F' traffic (Newcastle, Hull and Middlesbrough) was heavy, the 1.50pm Bursledon–Willesden Junction special vans called at Clapham Junction to detach vans in that group, which were forwarded on the extreme rear of the 6.45pm to Blackfriars. How they went forward from Blackfriars to the ER was not shown, but presumably this was via the LTE Widened Lines. The first service using a freight train was to be found that year when, if required, Swanwick had to provide and label a van 'Waterloo transfer' and attach this to the 7.25am freight from Bevois Park Sidings to Fareham, leaving Swanwick at 12.33pm and going

forward from Fareham as far as Eastleigh on the 1.3pm Portsmouth & Southsea–Salisbury and from Eastleigh on the 1.5pm Bournemouth West–Waterloo.

For 1954 there was quite a revamp of the notice contents, which also made for easier reading and understanding! It started as usual with the special instructions as explained for the 1951 publication but included an additional paragraph concerning wire trays. Was this method of carrying strawberries an innovation? Such trays, though, could only be used to convey traffic for Waterloo, Kew Bridge and South Wales stations. Perhaps individual customers had made specific requirements as otherwise we can conclude the previous arrangement was in wooden or paper punnets or trugs. Destination stations were instructed to return these trays promptly to the loading stations, with those from South Wales being loaded into an additional van when required labelled to Fareham and attached on to the rear of the 10.30am Cardiff General–Portsmouth & Southsea. Fareham had to detach the van and redistribute trays to stations as required. No guidance was given as to how empty trays from Waterloo and Kew Bridge were to be returned.

Then followed the definition of traffic groups and a further new feature which was termed a 'loading key', applicable for Mondays to Fridays. This detailed service numbers in the notice, where information was to be found for conveyance of traffic from all loading stations to individual stations in the aforementioned groups, with traffic divided into small, light or heavy categories. Loading stations remained the same as listed earlier in this article although forwarding was never resumed from Droxford (another Meon Valley station immediately north of Wickham) but, interestingly, Dunbridge was added. Fruit from this station was only to Group 'B' stations, ie Bristol and South Wales, being forwarded on the 4.45pm Portsmouth &

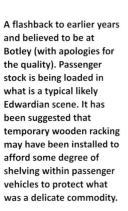
A flashback to earlier years and believed to be at Botley (with apologies for the quality). Passenger stock is being loaded in what is a typical likely Edwardian scene. It has been suggested that temporary wooden racking may have been installed to afford some degree of shelving within passenger vehicles to protect what was a delicate commodity.

Southsea–Salisbury for transfer at the latter station to the 5.37pm Portsmouth & Southsea–Cardiff General which did not call at Dunbridge. Bristol traffic was shown as destined for Temple Meads, not served by the 5.37pm ex-Portsmouth & Southsea, which instead was routed by and called at Stapleton Road. Presumably the Western Region (WR) transferred Bristol traffic at a station *en route* – no doubt Westbury – into a train which served Temple Meads.

Then followed a 'Train Arrangements' summary in time order of all additional trains and any consequential revision to other services including empty stock, light engine and freight, together with 'Q' pathways. Likely this made the whole notice easier to comprehend rather than the hotch potch arrangement used hitherto. To use modern terminology, it was more 'user friendly'. (Might this be as a result of mis-routings in previous years and subsequent claims for produce which had 'spoiled' as a result – Ed?) Individual pathway timings followed for all special trains and revisions. The same 1954 train plan closely followed previous years but some variations are noteworthy. For instance, vans via King's Cross in groups 'C' and 'F' (the North East and Scotland) were in 1951 worked to Waterloo on the 11.2am Bournemouth West–Waterloo and then tripped back to Clapham Junction. It was only if the train length including the additional vans exceeded platform capacity at Waterloo that they were detached at Basingstoke. However, by 1954 it was the practice always to make a detachment at Basingstoke, after which they were attached to the rear of the 1.33pm Basingstoke–Waterloo, which stopped specially at Clapham Junction to detach them. (Slightly surprisingly, the 11.2am did not adopt the same practice.)

An unusual factor made this train (the 1.33pm) a curiosity as, Fridays excepted, it ran normally up the main line but was routed via the up main loop platform for the detachment to be made. On Fridays only it was diverted via East Putney, so arriving on the Windsor line side of Clapham Junction. Advertised arrival time at Waterloo of this train was 2.51pm, but whichever route it ran by the additional Clapham Junction stop was not advertised and this was emphasised by an instruction to that effect. There was no instruction to the effect that prominent notice should be given to the public of revised arrival times at Waterloo, which were 2.56pm Fridays excepted and 3.7pm Fridays only. Use made of the 6.45pm Clapham Junction–Blackfriars service was not repeated in 1954 but the 2.32pm trip Victoria–Clapham Junction, introduced the previous year, was continued.

There followed full details of special van formations, arrangements for conveyance of vans other than through special van trains and instructions regarding the conveyance of small quantities of fruit in train vans of ordinary passenger services. A further new feature was a comprehensive summary of additional shunting engine provision. These were provided at Botley, Eastleigh, Fareham (three), Swanwick (two), Southampton Central and Southampton Terminus. With one exception, all engines were required during the afternoon and early evening, the exception being Swanwick where one of the two engines was required between 10.10am and 1.50pm.

Prior to 1954, arrangements in notices centred on Monday–Friday arrangements and it must be concluded that weekend arrangements appeared on SNs. The year 1954 was different by including arrangements for these two days when traffic forwarding was much lower than during the week. Maybe this situation partly arose from the fact that in those days shops were not open on Sundays but it is interesting to consider when taking into account that the fruit itself did not take a 'day off' from its ripening process!

The first empty van train shown in the notices appears on Saturdays in 1954, the 4.58am Waterloo–Clapham Junction no doubt consisting of vehicles received during the night. There were just two special van trains on Saturdays, the first the 5.0am 'Q' Clapham Junction–Kew Bridge which, if required to run, was to start at 4.45am. This train conveyed traffic off the Fridays 7.10pm Woolston–Waterloo but did not run if there were less than four vans, in which event the traffic was circulated via Waterloo. The second special train was the 7.55pm Swanwick–Fareham with Kew Bridge traffic for attachment at Fareham at 8.31pm to the 8.3pm ex-Portsmouth & Southsea together with a van off the 6.27pm Southampton Central–Portsmouth & Southsea with traffic from Woolston, Netley and Bursledon. This ensemble transferred at Eastleigh to the 7.55pm Bournemouth West–Waterloo vans. For this special from Swanwick, a light engine left Fratton at 6.40pm and upon arrival at Swanwick performed necessary shunting movements before working the train forward to Fareham and making the attachment to the train from Portsmouth. The engine then returned light to Fratton, departing Fareham at 8.45pm. Saturday movements to Glasgow St Enoch comprised traffic from Brockenhurst which reached Romsey by ordinary services and then on the 4.36pm Southampton Terminus–Cheltenham Spa (Lansdown) via the MSWJ, plus a van (or vans) from Swanwick on the 12.33pm Portsmouth & Southsea–Southampton Terminus where attachment was made to the 4.36pm service to Cheltenham.

On Sundays there was only one special van train, the 4.15am Clapham Junction–Kew Bridge with vans off the previous day's 7.55pm Bournemouth West–Waterloo vans. Nevertheless, with Waterloo transfer traffic vans left Swanwick on ordinary services at 2.3pm (1.26pm Portsmouth & Southsea–Southampton Central), from where an attachment was made to the 3.24pm Southampton Central–Waterloo. To make this transfer an engine was required at Southampton Central between 2.45pm and 3.15pm.

Two further van movements were made from Swanwick with Waterloo traffic. The first was at 5.00pm to Southampton Central on the 4.26pm Portsmouth & Southsea–Southampton Central from where it went forward as far as Basingstoke at 6.41pm on the 5.18pm Bournemouth West–Basingstoke and from Basingstoke at 10.2pm on the 8.3pm Portsmouth & Southsea–Waterloo – a through train from Portsmouth & Southsea to Waterloo via Eastleigh. The final such working departed Swanwick at 5.51pm on the 4.55pm Southampton Central–Portsmouth & Southsea and meandered through to Portsmouth & Southsea from where it continued its journey on the previously mentioned 8.3pm to Waterloo. There was no provision at Swanwick for shunting engines to attach vans to these three services, so they must have been on trains from starting stations and loaded rapidly upon arrival.

In 1955 through vans were loaded for Glasgow on Fridays 1, 15 and 29 July and with specific instructions these had to be labelled to 'Glasgow High Street'. Was this because of annual Glasgow holidays? A new empty van train on weekdays also appeared in the notice, the 8.30am Southampton New Docks (as the present Western Docks were called then) to Swanwick, calling at Netley and Bursledon if required to detach.

Picking time!

On Saturdays the following alterations were made to the workings of the previous year's van trains: 4.58am Waterloo–Clapham Junction and 5.0am 'Q' Clapham Junction–Kew Bridge both discontinued and the 7.55pm Swanwick–Fareham now started from Netley at 7.30pm, also calling at Bursledon. Vans from Botley to Glasgow departed from Botley at 4.22pm on the 3.45pm Portsmouth & Southsea–Romsey, going forward from Romsey on the 4.36pm Southampton Terminus–Cheltenham Spa (Lansdown). Shunting engines were provided when required at Fareham, Swanwick and Netley. Vans for Glasgow St Enoch from Brockenhurst and Romsey were worked on ordinary services to Romsey and those from Swanwick to Southampton Terminus, all for the 4.36pm Southampton Terminus to Cheltenham Spa (Lansdown). Kew Bridge traffic was worked on ordinary services from Botley and Netley line stations to Eastleigh for the 7.55pm Bournemouth West–Waterloo vans, which were detached at Clapham Junction for the 4.15am (Sundays) special vans Clapham Junction–Kew Bridge. Whilst no special van trains ran on Sundays, some vans from Swanwick passed by ordinary services as in 1954.

For the years 1956 and 1957, as in 1955, on some Fridays in July vans for Glasgow St Enoch were labelled to Glasgow High Street Goods. Apart from that there were only minor variations.

In 1958, this year's notice was very different and contained just 10 pages only compared with 22 pages the previous year. The Hampshire DEMUs had been introduced in September 1957, so this was the first summer of their operation. Not surprisingly, the fruit programme differed considerably from previous years with, for instance, some ordinary services that had previously been used, now having disappeared. The loading key was also omitted, forwardings from Dunbridge ceased and LTE Widened Lines trains also disappeared. Why these alterations occurred is

not clear but it is unlikely to be directly related to the later closure of the Widened Lines, which came about just over a decade later. Probably it was due to other factors involved, outside the scope of this article, possibly associated with growers no longer planting strawberries or a move away from rail.

Meanwhile the traffic Groups were amended. Group 'A' was Aberdeen, Edinburgh, Hull and Middlesbrough. Group 'B' was Glasgow St Enoch (forwardings to Glagow on Fridays in July were labelled as per recent years, viz to Glasgow Central); Group 'C' (via London) was traffic to Accrington, Blackpool, Blackburn, Burnley, Carlisle, Liverpool (Lime Street), Manchester (London Road), Southport and Huddersfield. Group 'D' was Bristol (Temple Meads), Cardiff (General), Ebbw Vale, Haverfordwest, Merthyr Tydfil, Neath, Newport (Mon), Port Talbot, Swansea, Tonyrefail. Group 'E' was London (Waterloo), and finally Group 'F' was Kew Bridge.

With no opportunity now to add vehicles to existing local passenger workings, special van trains were run, namely: 11.31am Swanwick–Southampton Central which conveyed Edinburgh traffic only from Swanwick and Bursledon, attached at Southampton Central to the 11.16am Bournemouth West–Newcastle; 12.42pm Netley–Eastleigh via Fareham with traffic in groups A, B and C for Waterloo transfer, transferred at Eastleigh to the 2.32pm to Waterloo (1.5pm ex-Bournemouth West); 2.0pm Bursledon–Willesden Junction via Fareham, Eastleigh, Woking, East Putney, Clapham Junction and Kensington Olympia with traffic in groups B and C from Bursledon, Swanwick and Botley; 5.40pm Botley–Romsey with South Wales traffic attached to the 5.45pm Portsmouth & Southsea–Cardiff General at Romsey; 8.20pm Southampton Terminus–Southampton Central with traffic from Netley line stations for Waterloo and Kew Bridge which had arrived at Southampton Terminus on the 6.8pm Portsmouth & Southsea–Salisbury vans via Southampton Terminus and Eastleigh. This had vans which had departed from Swanwick at 7.30pm. At Southampton Central these vans were forwarded on the 6.30pm Weymouth–Waterloo. The 6.8pm ex-Portsmouth & Southsea vans also carried fruit from Botley, which unusually was conveyed by railway cartage to Swanwick.

There were no special van trains to the WR via Salisbury and Westbury; instead, any vans were conveyed on the 5.8pm Portsmouth & Southsea–Southampton Central stopping service which continued as empty stock to Romsey where vans were attached to the 5.45pm Portsmouth & Southsea–Cardiff General. The 5.8pm ex-Portsmouth & Southsea was introduced as part of the Hampshire diesel scheme but it was a steam train until 4 January 1960, by which time more DEMUs had become available. Also, on Mondays–Fridays no traffic now circulated via Andover Junction and Cheltenham. Glasgow traffic from the Lymington branch and Brockenhurst passed on the 1.5pm Bournemouth West–Waterloo as far as Eastleigh, from where it went forward on the 2.0pm Bursledon–Willesden Junction special van train. Fruit from Brockenhurst to Kew Bridge went on the 6.30pm Weymouth–Waterloo. No reference was made with regard to traffic from Kent, which was worked from Victoria to Clapham Junction. Perhaps this was conveyed on a direct Victoria–Willesden Junction service.

Additional shunting engines were required during various afternoon periods at Fareham, Basingstoke and Waterloo. An additional empty van train ran leaving Southampton New Docks for Swanwick at 9.15am.

On Saturdays, whilst no special van trains were run, traffic for Edinburgh Princes Street and Glasgow Central departed Brockenhurst at 12.33pm (10.10 Weymouth–Waterloo stopper) to Eastleigh, from where they went forward to Southampton Terminus at 3.27pm on the 12.42pm Didcot–Southampton Terminus, and from there on the 4.50pm Southampton Terminus–Cheltenham Spa (Lansdown). But there was a snag in that the 12.42 ex-Didcot was discontinued from 7 July 1958 – as was later established, a definite pre-closure run-down prior to closure in 1960. Revised arrangements would therefore have been required to work these vans between Eastleigh and Southampton Terminus which were no doubt published in weekly 'P' notices or on a 'SN'. The 4.50pm ex-Southampton Terminus also conveyed traffic originating from Swanwick, which had now arrived by road – railway cartage – to Southampton Terminus. The 7.18pm Portsmouth & Southsea–Eastleigh parcels also included a fruit van for Waterloo transferred at Eastleigh to our by now familiar friend, the 7.55pm Bournemouth West–Waterloo vans containing traffic destined for Kew Bridge.

Meanwhile traffic from Netley line stations for the 7.18 ex-Portsmouth & Southsea parcels, had to be spread over diesel services (due to their limited luggage space in the brake vans) to Fareham for transfer there.

Sundays saw three special van trains running, the first the 4.5am Waterloo–Kew Bridge handling traffic received on various Saturday night/Sunday morning services. The other two specials were both from Swanwick to Eastleigh via Fareham (reverse of course) calling at Botley with vans for Waterloo, departing at 1.15pm and then 5.10pm and at Eastleigh attaching to the 3.50pm (3.37pm ex-Southampton Central) and at 6.55pm (5.15pm ex-Bournemouth West) to Waterloo respectively. At Waterloo, shunting engines were required to detach these vans.

When comparing 1959 with 1958, it is apparent the annual revisions indicated a decrease in traffic was expected. The number of destination stations in the various groups had gone down with the following now omitted: Group 'C' via London – Accrington, Blackpool, Blackburn, Burnley, Carlisle and Southport. Group 'D': Bristol (Temple Meads), Haverfordwest, Neath, Port Talbot and Tonyrefail but Tonypandy was added. It is not known whether this reduction was the result of station closures, reduction of handling facilities at stations or a switch to road conveyance, but most likely it was the latter as it would seem strange to report otherwise that the consumption of fruit had diminished. Nevertheless, at this time there was also a general reduction of rail services although this was before the advent of Beeching. Notwithstanding all that was going on, the only special van train casualty was the 12.42pm Netley–Eastleigh, now starting from Swanwick at 1.10pm, and the afternoon shunting engine was also withdrawn. The Fridays only late June and mid July requirement for Glasgow vans to be labelled to Glasgow High Street Goods was also changed to

Glasgow Eglington Street Parcels Depot. Another change was the 9.15am empty van train from Southampton New Docks–Swanwick which was revised to start at 8.40am. Once again, no reference was made to Kent-originating traffic even though Phase 1 of the Kent Coast electrification was introduced that year.

It will be recalled that use of the 4.50pm Southampton Terminus–Cheltenham Spa (Lansdown) in 1958 was restricted to Saturdays but this changed in 1959 by making use of the DNS line and sending such vans via Newbury! This came about following diversion of the 4.50pm ex-Southampton Terminus to Cheltenham Spa (St James) following removal of the connection between WR and LMR lines outside Lansdown and so enabling trains to run to that station. These vans assembled at Southampton Terminus for attachment to the Cheltenham train, which then had to be worked to Eastleigh for attachment to the 5.15pm Eastleigh–Didcot and subsequent detachment at Newbury. The notice gives no clue as to subsequent services from Newbury. There were no changes to the 1958 Sunday workings.

So to 1960 and the final year of this review. The year produced a season with many service revisions, a number intended to divert traffic off the West Coast main line as electrification work there gained momentum. The front cover page of the notice included a note to the effect that it now included certain items relating to Kent fruit traffic via the London junctions. Opening special instructions included a paragraph regarding van restrictions which stated that vehicles for Glasgow, Edinburgh and Liverpool (Lime Street) had to be bogie vans not over 9ft 3in wide whilst Manchester (Oldham Road) could only accept four-wheeled passenger vans provided they were not over that same width.

Some Groups were again revised, with Group 'A' consisting of Aberdeen and Edinburgh only and Group 'C' expanded to include Hull, Newcastle, Leicester, Derby and Leeds but with Huddersfield deleted. Groups 'B', 'D', 'E' and' F' were unaltered. Kent rejoined the picture but with its own groups, Group 'B' meaning Glasgow, Group 'C': Liverpool (Lime Street) and Manchester (Oldham Road) and a new Group 'K' for Bristol, Cardiff, Coventry, Birmingham and Wolverhampton.

Special van trains ran as follows:

* 11.31am Swanwick–Southampton Central for Edinburgh only and attached to the 11.16am Bournemouth West–Newcastle.

* 12.2pm Swanwick–Eastleigh via Fareham with fruit in Group 'B'. This was a complicated working starting from Eastleigh formed of a 3 corr set (the normal 12.53pm Eastleigh-Reading General stock) and upon arrival at Swanwick the engine worked the 11.31am vans, but vans were attached to the 3 corr set with the whole entourage forming the 12.2 pm train. But another engine was required for the 12.2pm which arrived light from Eastleigh, pausing *en route* to do a spot of shunting at Botley again to collect any vans from here. This was not the end of the saga as upon arrival at Fareham the original 12.2pm engine promptly

worked the Meon Valley freight to Droxford at 12.35pm. Meanwhile a turnover engine had arrived at Fareham and worked the train to Eastleigh from where both passenger stock and vans formed the 12.53pm to Reading General. Complicated? I would say so!

* 2.10pm Swanwick–Eastleigh via Fareham with traffic in Group 'C', attached at Eastleigh to the 3.7pm Portsmouth & Southsea-Reading General for detachment at Basingstoke to form a 4.50pm special to Clapham Junction via East Putney.

* 5.5pm Botley–Southampton Central via Fareham with fruit in Group 'D', attached at Southampton Central to the 5.45pm Portsmouth & Southsea–Cardiff General.

* 8.20pm Southampton Terminus–Southampton Central with fruit in Groups 'E' and 'F' with traffic from Swanwick off the 6.15pm Portsmouth & Southsea–Salisbury via Southampton Terminus and Eastleigh parcels which departed Swanwick at 7.30pm, and attached to 6.30pm Weymouth–Waterloo at Southampton Central.

So much for the unusual and if those were thought different, here are the real gems:

* 2.55pm Victoria–Hendon via Barnes, Kew East Junction and Brent No 2 Junction conveying traffic from Victoria and calling at Clapham Junction to pick up van(s) for Glasgow off the 12.58pm Salisbury–Waterloo, of which see also later.

* 3.35pm Waterloo–Hendon by the same route conveying Glasgow traffic which had worked to Waterloo also on the 12.58pm ex-Salisbury. An SR engine worked this train throughout but with a conductor driver from Brent No 2 Junction, although it was noted the guard worked only as far as that junction.

* 6.8pm Hither Green–Clapham Junction (arrive 6.40pm) with Kent traffic in Groups 'C' and 'K'. Possibly the necessity for this train arose following the introduction the previous year of Kent Coast electrification Phase 1.

* 7.29pm Clapham Junction–Woodford Halse – there was still life in the Great Central main line – with vans from Hampshire and Kent and traffic destined for the Midlands and Northern destinations in Group 'C', plus Kent traffic to Bristol and Cardiff detached at Kensington Olympia for transfer to the WR

With further regard to the 12.58pm and 4.5pm Salisbury–Waterloo, both trains were diverted via East Putney to detach on the Windsor lines at Clapham Junction. It will be recalled that the former train had vans attached at Basingstoke off the 12.53pm ex-Eastleigh and the latter train also had vans attached at Basingstoke but this time off the 3.7pm Portsmouth & Southsea-Reading General, all for the 7.29pm to Woodford Halse. Concerning both the trains from Salisbury, as in previous years there was no suggestion that passengers should be advised of the revised arrival time at Waterloo whilst again, as before, the notice instruction stated that the Clapham Junction stops were not to be advertised.

Empty vans for Swanwick and Fareham this year were conveyed on an 8.40pm special from Southampton Old Docks as the Eastern Docks were then known.

On Saturdays, traffic this year was for Glasgow only from Swanwick – once more conveyed by railway cartage to Southampton Terminus – and also from Brockenhurst. But the DNS line's season of glory the previous year conveying such vans was not to be repeated this time, any vans now being worked from Southampton Terminus to Eastleigh for attachment to the 8.30pm Eastleigh–Waterloo normal empty van train and detached at Clapham Junction, going forward from there by the 3.0am (Sunday morning) to Willesden Junction. On Sundays the only alteration to 1959 arrangements was that the 4.5am Waterloo–Kew Bridge vans did not run.

Swanwick, probably in pre-Grouping days, with strawberry loading in progress. It may also be noted that ordinary goods traffic was not neglected. Of particular interest is the boarding and notices on the end of the vans nearest the camera – the wording of which is unfortunately not quite decipherable. Might this even be instructions as to which van was for which destination? *Tony Sedgwick/Ian Wilkins*

Summer at Swanwick, but this time post-1960 and now without a single strawberry. The yard here finally closed in 1972, the other principal location referred to in the text, Botley, had lost its yard the year before, 1971, although it is unlikely that either had seen much, if any, traffic for some time previously. It is worth mentioning that associated with the movement of soft fruit from the area was the Swanwick and District Fruit Growers' Association, founded in 1905 and which in 1913 opened a basket-making cooperative. The basket factory employed mainly women in the manufacturing process. By 1949 over 60 people worked at the site but this number had dropped to just six by 1964 as new materials in punnet manufacture were introduced. We should also not forget that other areas away from the Southern had a reputation for strawberry traffic, the GWR Cheddar Valley line in Somerset also sometimes being referred to as the 'Strawberry Line'. *S. W. C. Eyers collection*

In conclusion, we may state that the special traffic 'P' notices contained all the arrangements required to convey this traffic, whether by special van trains or ordinary services. Obviously every arrangement did not operate every day; it really was a case of selecting which arrangement would operate according to traffic requirements. Who actually decided when traffic was light or heavy, I do not know, but it is likely that the growers had some sort of committee who forecast traffic levels, having close liaison with Southampton District Office special traffic section. Not to be overlooked is the role played by Eastleigh Passenger Rolling Stock section, which was responsible for procuring sufficient numbers of empty vans. In that era, vans still came in all sorts of shapes and sizes and had to be sourced to be within the confines of such lines as the LTE Widened lines. Also, there were the equally important people 'on the ground' to make it all work. Local Station Masters of the time must have pored over these notices for many hours, deciding what was required locally from them, and the staff on their patch, to make it all happen. Headaches were bound to have arisen from time to time! If I have omitted to mention anybody (or a section) who had an integral part to play in this military precision-type operation, then I apologise.

So, to sum up, whilst the special traffic notices were very detailed and consequently complex, perusing them has been most interesting, evoking many memories of past times. I would, perhaps hold back *(for the moment – ED…?)* from undertaking a similar exercise on the Christmas mails and parcels special traffic notice; now, they were beasts!

Finally, by coincidence, whilst compiling this article, I received my copy of the October 2016 edition of 'South Western Circular' volume 17 No 4, published by the South Western Circle. It included an article entitled 'Hampshire Strawberries and the London & South Western Railway' written by J. Thornton Burge and originally published in the *Railway and Travel Monthly* in 1915. Suffice it to say, comparison between those days and the decade reviewed in this article is both interesting and absorbing!

Abbreviations used in this article:

DNS – Didcot, Newbury & Southampton Railway

ER – Eastern Region

L&NWR – London & North Western Railway

L&Y – Lancashire & Yorkshire Railway

LMR – London Midland Region

LTE – London Transport Executive

MSWJ – Midland and South Western Junction Railway

'P' Notices – Special Traffic Working weekly printed notices; also issued to cover other special events.

'Q' – Pathway for working that runs if required

SN – Daily issued special traffic working notice typed on stencil

SR – Southern Region

WR – Western Region

Not guaranteed to be related to strawberries, but a light engine movement, Class 4 No 80066, on the Netley line, is seen here at the station of the same name and recorded 'wrong road' with the dummy off to enter the yard. Dare we consider it might have been sent to collect vans of soft fruit…? *Roger Thornton*

The Lost Archives of Stephen Townroe
Part 4

This latest part of the archive commences at Yeovil sometime soon after October 1938, where Stephen Townroe (SCT) had been moved to in April 1939. Notwithstanding the deteriorating international situation, SCT saw to it that standards had to be maintained, as witness the condition of the engines he recorded here. The photographs in this instalment will take us through to the start of World War 2 and include some examples of the British Expeditionary Force on their way to France as well as his own move to a headquarters role and the difficulties associated with the running of electric trains in the very cold winter of 1940.

The next instalment in this fascinating series commences with the wartime offices at Deepdene, before looking at several aspects of wartime working around the Southern. None of the images to be published will have been seen before.

'U' class No 1790 being cleaned on Yeovil shed. The embellishment in the centre of the smokebox will be noted. Whether this was preparation for a special train was not reported.

Right: SCT has this and two almost identical images referred to as 'the engine that failed', possibly a reference to the apparent sad look of the cab spectacles. Whether this was simply his interpretation of the look portrayed, or as was also included in his index entry, the words 'comic strip' and therefore part of something else, we cannot know. Whatever the meaning, it is clearly a clean 'T9' with detail of the snifting valves and smokebox clamps, the latter in addition to the more normal central fastening. This was also recorded at Yeovil.

Below and bottom: Two views now of the inside of the shed including the cleaning out of the pits. The interior brickwork was painted white with the deliberate intention of creating as bright a working environment as possible, although as the lighting was probably gas, maintenance at night – and later under blackout conditions – could not have been easy. The individual engines are not all identified by number.

Above: The inside of the shed offices with clerk R. Bartlett hard at work (he would have to be, with the boss present!).

Left and below: The exterior hoist in operation, receiving attention is 'O2' No 187. Two members of the class, No 187 and No 207, both motor fitted, had been transferred to Yeovil in February 1939 to replace 'D1' class engines on the Yeovil Junction–Yeovil Town shuttle. The duty also included a single early morning turn to Templecombe and a late evening visit to Yeovil Pen Mill.

Occasionally Yeovil might be called upon to assist the 'opposition' when things they would rather have kept quiet about occurred. Such an example took place at Chard Junction (SCT does not give an exact date) when Townroe's men succeeded in re-railing GWR 2-6-2T No 4581 'off all-wheels' in just two hours twenty minutes. The circumstances of the derailment are not given. It was experience gained in re-railing situations such as this that would be of such use later in his career. No 4581 was likely a Taunton (GWR-based) engine and was fitted with a tablet catcher for working trains on the Minehead branch.

Opposite and overleaf: On 22 June 1939 King George VI and Queen Elizabeth returned to Southampton following a tour of the USA and Canada. Returning them to London, a special train of Pullman cars was used hauled by 'Lord Nelson' No 851 *Sir Francis Drake*. SCT was there but whether in an official capacity is not certain. Whatever the reason, he recorded the service working 'wrong road' on the approach to Southampton and then similarly leaving from what was in effect Platform 4. Notice the flagmen necessary for such a move. For the record, Driver Blaney and Inspector Watson are on the footplate.

Left: Sunday overtime perhaps, with fitters working on *King Arthur* No 453. At the time this was a Salisbury-based engine but was clearly in need of attention before returning to its home depot.

Below and below left: These two views are simply referred to as 'Trains at Templecombe'. That seen approaching is a train from the direction of Salisbury, which is then seen again from the rear. Next stop Milborne Port perhaps? The locomotive is 'N15' No 789 *Sir Guy*.

The wartime book *Junction X* has previously been mentioned in earlier editions and special issues of SW giving as it does an excellent representation of traffic movement at a necessarily fictitious junction during wartime. What was not known nor recorded in this July 1944 paperback was that one of SCT's images was used, although naturally without the location being identified. It was in fact taken at Yeovil Junction during shunting movement early one morning and actually recorded in the period prior to June 1940, thus a few years prior to publication. Locomotive details are not given.

Morale boosting comments being chalked on to the side of a coach at Yeovil Junction as early as July 1939. The originating station and train destination are not stated, although SCT refers to it as the 'BEF leaving for France'.

January 1940 was not a good time for the Southern. Extreme temperature lows, in many places the coldest since the previous century, added to occasional precipitation, created the conditions for an ice storm around the 20th of the month. At several electric depots the units were literally frozen to the rails. At this unnamed location an attempt was first made to chip away the ice by hand before the final ignominy of having to revert to steam so that some services at least might operate. In image 57 the locomotive heading a 2BIL unit is '700' class 0-6-0 No 692.

Rebuilt
The Letters and Comments Pages

As always, very many thanks to all who have sent in comments, queries and questions. In no particular order, we start with a question from Graham Biggles, 'Where and when did trials with the lightweight ACV diesel sets take place on the Southern. And, what was the last loco to carry "Southern" livery?' Well, the first question we can answer courtesy of the two images above which have just been located.

Above: **The first photograph shows the lightweight ACV diesel set at Newbury after having reached there from Didcot – further details in the text. The second is that referred to by R. C. Riley, taken at Cliffe but with apologies for what is a print not up to the usual Dick Riley standard.**

Graham sent these queries to us by email and we have responded to the effect that so far as the ACV sets are concerned we know they ran their very first trial not far from the Southern, that is between Didcot and Newbury, around 28 April 1952, after which trials and services were operated by the London Midland Region (LMR) mainly in the London area. According to http://www.railcar.co.uk/type/acv/operations, the only trials on the Southern took place on the Allhallows branch sometime in late October 1953 – unless of course you know differently! (There is a photograph by the late R. C. Riley of the ACV set at Cliffe on 24 October. It appeared within the OPC book *Branches and Byways – Kent*.)

Earlier correspondence from Graham Biggles had referred to the articulated sets built from the coach portions of the former South Eastern & Chatham Railway (SECR) steam railmotors. Here we see one of these sets at Leysdown, loco-hauled by 'B1' 4-4-0 No 1021. Mike King provides the full answer to the use of vehicles, 'There were just two SR 2-coach sets converted from SECR railmotor trailers in 1924 and used on the Sheppey Light Railway until it closed in 1950. After that the two sets (SR 513 and 514) led a somewhat nomadic existence for a few years, appearing at Weymouth–Portland–Easton, Hayling Island, Exmouth and then Kensington Olympia for a few years before ending their days about 1959 on the Fawley branch. At least one set was in lined crimson during that time.' *Crecy Transport Heritage Library/LGRP/NRM*

Graham's second query might be answered from an image (regretfully too poor to be reproduced) which appeared on page 156 of the *British Railways Magazine – Southern Region* for August 1955. It depicts a 'W' class 2-6-4T No 31916 at Hither Green in June 1954 (the years 1955 and 1954 are correct) carrying a BR smokebox plate at least but with the word 'Southern' clearly displayed on the tankside. Unfortunately, the poor quality does not allow confirmation of whether a BR number was shown on the bunker side. The caption states 'The last "Southern" tank engine …', with the image submitted by A. Earle Edwards (a name I recall from the 1960s). Can anyone confirm if this was indeed the last 'Southern' engine?

Now a correction – with thanks – from Roger MacDonald, 'What a glorious piece of colour nostalgia *In the Summer of '45* was! On page 109 (SW37) I think you will find that PS *Monarch* is tied up at Swanage, not Bournemouth Pier. I was lucky to have many a trip on her, especially the evening cruise from Bournemouth to Poole via Swanage. On departing from Swanage it was the practice to block off part of the passageway down below; cinders and ash would be hoisted up in skips from the boiler room and deposited over the side, to be churned up by the paddle wheels. There is probably still a trail of the stuff right across Swanage Bay towards Old Harry Rocks!'

Next some additional information from Adrian Westbury on the subject of Holmwood and the GWR railcar depicted at Southampton – again 'SW37': 'Thanks for yet another interesting and varied volume. I would comment on two items, observations and memories:

'Page 25 upper. Nice to see a photograph of Holmwood station. I used it from September 1948 until July 1952 to go to and from Dorking North for school, catching the 8.31am in the morning and returning on the 4.23pm or, if we missed it, the 5.01. One of the highlights each month was to purchase my copy of the *Railway Magazine* from the bookstall at Dorking North.

'I used the station again from August 1952 until August 1955, catching that roundabout train which ran from London Bridge to Brighton and taking, from memory, almost three and a half hours for the journey. I recall it was something like 6.30 am at Holmwood. I only caught it on Monday mornings to go to Brighton Works, where I was an apprentice; in "digs" the rest of the week. You may recall I sent you an article on my recollections of time there some time ago. *(Indeed, included with grateful thanks in this issue – Ed.)*

'Another memory of Holmwood during my school days was that my father was one of the porters and Don Wilson was the signalman on the same shift. When working on late turn Saturday evenings, Don cooked up a supper for both in the signal box, usually sausage, beans and egg, and I would walk the mile from home to join them – and to pull off a few levers. The pull for the down distant was hard, much more so than the equivalent for the up line. Don used to tip me off when one of the weekly Special notices showed an excursion from another region to Littlehampton or Bognor, invariably hauled by a Maunsell Mogul. Some Saturdays the Norwood–Chichester freight might also be routed that way with one of the electric locos in charge.

'Page 94: The photograph of the GWR railcar could not have been in connection with the 1947 trials you mention as it appears to be in carmine and cream not chocolate and

Reference our recent piece in SW36 on the 'glass house' signal box designs, Greg Beecroft has kindly sent us this view of Wimbledon 'A' which ceased operation in 1991. Although nearby Woking and Horsham boxes are now listed by English Heritage as 'Grade 2', no such protection exists for Wimbledon and as such its long-term future must be questionable.

Fresh from overhaul, 'G6' 0-6-0T No DS3152 is seen being shunted at Eastleigh prior to running in and then subsequent return to its home base of Meldon Quarry. This engine was employed at the Devon site from November 1949 until July 1960.

cream. Also, in GWR days the roundel insignia was carried each end just above the tail lamp bracket. Counting the windows it would appear to be one in the No 7–16 batch.'

Received by Royal Mail from Roy White: 'Having just read SW37, I have a couple of comments to make. Alan Postlethwaite asks why station names are repeated on single tickets? I worked at Blandford Forum as a booking clerk from 1956–61, leaving then because the Western Region was getting a bit too close! Anyway, should a child need a single ticket, it was cut (not the child) in half diagonally from bottom left corner to top right hand corner using the left half as the child's single at half the price. If you had a second child that day, the right half could then be used, which still showed the journey details. If at the end of the day we had sold an odd number of halves the odd half ticket was retained to account for what would otherwise be a shortage of cash.

'In the same issue Richard Simmons states that only one freight train travelled in the down direction between Brockenhurst and Hamworthy Junction. This is not strictly true as the 5.55am freight from Evercreech Junction to Hamworthy Junction travelled this line, arriving at HJ at 8.00am and departing 45 minutes later tender first to Poole where the engine was now facing the right way to take the 9.20am freight to Templecombe. On the way north it recessed into Carter's siding near Corfe Mullen between 9.42am and 10.47am. This was necessary so it could be got out of the way of the up "Pines". The freight was worked by an S&D 2-8-0, the only time one of these was seen south of Templecombe other than on a summer Saturday. The diagram was a three-day cycle leaving

Bath at 5.50am on the first day and not returning to Bath until 11.45pm on day three. The two intervening nights being spent on Templecombe shed.'

Now from Vic Freemantle on the subject of Brockenhurst and Woodfidley – p15 'SW37': 'Hello Kevin. By coincidence checking old copies of the *Railway Modeller* for plans of Brockenhurst goods shed, I found the following letter in the January 1980 issue on the area from a G. Kinsey in response to an article on those LSWR keepers' cottages. Whilst it may not be unknown by your present author I include the relevant part of his letter which you can decide if or not it helps.

"I believe Mr Ormiston-Chant has also erred in describing Woodfidley Crossing as unique. I suspect that the S&T department, having established the need for an intermediate signal box in the area, simply took the opportunity of placing it next to a formerly remote and potentially dangerous level crossing. Many examples existed. Although it appears to have been rebuilt at some stage, Woodfidley box originally opened in August 1884. This information was obtained from LSWR circulars, dating from the 1880s which survived in Brockenhurst Station Manager's office until destroyed when the office was broken into and set alight by vandals.

"There is no mention or hint of there ever having been any form of platform/station there. *Track layouts of the SR, Section 2* by G. A. Pryer shows it as a signal box only. It closed on 23 October 1966 when the level crossing was reduced to Occupation status, presumably due to the pending electrification and consolidation of signal boxes."'

A piece here from Graham Buxton-Smither: 'Dear Kevin. Today was a bumper day as I received *Southern Way 37* and two of the volumes of the *Illustrated History of Southern Wagons* series. *(The whole series of Southern Wagons is something that should be on the shelves of all Southern enthusiasts – Ed.)*

'As always, *SW* gets my full attention and I was stopped in my tracks by the 2BIL piccie on p23 showing the unit at Reigate. What perplexed me was that the train was facing the wrong direction; after looking closely, given the building in the background, I'm fairly sure that the unit is on the platform for trains to Guildford and Reading although the absence of the footbridge over the level crossing surprised me. However, even if it was on the Redhill platform, it's still the wrong way round. And then I remembered that in the days before the "tadpole" units invaded the Tonbridge to Reading services, the 2BIL (for it was almost always one of those venerable units) that had arrived from Redhill would off-load its human cargo and the occasional parcel and then move forwards to the crossing on the Redhill side of the tracks before reversing into the other platform, ready for its onward journey to Redhill. The guard must already have prepared for this and that was why the headcode was showing on the unit at the "wrong end".

'Reigate was a slightly odd-ball station in that it was the terminus for third rail services but a through station for steam and, latterly and currently, diesel services to Reading. I used to travel from there to South Croydon via East Croydon every school-day from 1962 to 1969. Reigate had a small goods yard and some carriage sidings when I started travelling and I can recall the pleasure of watching an early morning 2-BIL coming directly from the carriage sidings to the platform as they always seemed "cleaner and more fresh" than the ones from Redhill. There was also the excitement of getting to Redhill and being joined to a Victoria or London Bridge service on Platform 1, waiting for that inevitable "bump" as the units coupled. I seem to recall that the Station Master was usually present when the man jumped down on to the rails between the trains and coupled them; there was also quite a kafuffle on the platform with a number of station staff and two guards trying to ensure that no one attempted to board as the Reigate portion bumped forward to enable the coupling; this was long before the days of remote locking and of course also in the days when all the stock had slam doors. It's wonderful how a small photo can rekindle so many memories.

'Thank you once again for a fabulous issue; I can't wait for April and your forthcoming article on the interchange trials …' *(Graham, thank you, I do hope you enjoyed that in SW38 – Ed.)*

We showed Graham's letter to the author of the article concerned, Alan Postlethwaite, who has responded, 'Graham knows more about the 2BILs at Reigate than I do. I rode the unit in question but I have no recollection of the reversing procedure. All I can add is the date of the photo, which is 17 August 1958. It was my very first photographic outing beyond London. I went on to photograph Dorking Town where the goods yard was integral with the station forecourt. Happy days!'

Variations in station name boards at Clapham Junction. This first view of the LBSCR type of board was photographed on the West London railway platform (17) in 1958. Next we have an LSWR/SR board, appropriately also with an LSWR engine in the background. The next three are of unknown company origin; they are likely to all date from SR days but also indicate that commonality was not always a priority! Again, all were recorded in 1958.

Jeremy Clarke now adds a view on the image on p20 (SW37): 'RE Sw37. Me again! The caption to the picture on p20 is a little misleading when it states that "All the EMUs built until 1932 were conversions …". Not quite. Fifty-five 3SUB sets, with LSWR 'torpedo'-style cabs, were built new in 1925, motor coaches by Birmingham CW, trailers by Midland RCW, Metrovick electrical gear. These were for the first installation of third-rail on the Eastern Section and the extension on the Western Section to Dorking and Guildford. The motors were of 300hp as opposed to the 275hp of previous sets. MCB automatic couplers fitted between the vehicles were later removed in favour of the usual semi-permanent three-link chains after proving unreliable.' *(That is an interesting comment in itself. By implication it suggests either the units would not couple or might even uncouple by themselves. Might anyone know the answer to this – Ed?)* Jeremy continues, 'Does anyone know if the 26 Western Section sets were numbered 1285–1310 and the 29 Easterns 1496–1524? The latter also had one extra compartment per coach, a reflection of the greater demand out of Victoria and Holborn Viaduct. Post-war, all were augmented to become 4SUB, and renumbered in a single series, 4301–4354. (It appears one Western set had gone AWOL but I have not been able to find out when or why. A wartime problem would seem the obvious conclusion.) These sets were remarkable for their longevity, not being withdrawn until 1959/61, although 10 pairs of Eastern Section motor coaches were rebuilt as de-icing units, Nos S92-101. Some if not all were still active to the end of the 1970s.

'Now reference the "WIM" sets pictured on pp26, 27 and 32. Fact is they are not "WIMs" but "SLs". The latter were rebuilt into eight sets from the original South London motor coaches to continue working the SLL after its conversion to dc in 1928. They were numbered 1901-8. The distinctive flattened roof end where the pantograph was placed is clear in all three photos. Moreover, it is No 1805 (ex-1905) pictured on pp26 and 30. I think it is also the one on p27 but cannot be sure. The four "WIM" sets were made up of eight original "SL" trailers, which had been converted to steam stock but were reconverted in 1930 on electrification of the West Croydon–Wimbledon line and numbered 1901-12. They featured the usual LSWR-style sloping roof over the driver's cab. All these coaches were 9ft 6in wide. The 12 sets, renumbered 1801-12 in 1934, were restricted to working on the lines for which they had been adapted, the "SLs" being maintained at Peckham Rye and the "WIMs" having dispensation to work to Selhurst for the purpose.

'The upper picture on p32 brought back some happy memories of daily travel on the "2 Trains" from West Croydon after my employers had shown unusual perception in transferring me from their branch in Upper Norwood to Wimbledon for a period of about 15 months. (The subsequent move to Chiswick wasn't nearly so welcome!) As I started this commute in 1959, the "WIMs" had given way to the rather less distinctive "2EPB" units. The comment about the track layout in the picture brings to mind that another – non-electrified – single track once paralleled the line between West Croydon and Beddington Lane Halt to serve Croydon's utilities and some extensive industrial sites *en route*. Much of this traffic emanated from Norwood Yard and the single slip enabled return traffic immediately to gain the up line thence. (The "WIMs" were also permitted to use it to get to Selhurst for maintenance.)

'By dint of some quick turn-rounds at both termini, there was a 20-minute interval West Croydon–Wimbledon rush-hour service in those days, made possible by trains usually passing one another on the ¾-mile double track section between Mitcham Junction and Mitcham. But it needed swift staff work by the signalmen to maintain it. (As a tip to the line's previous existence this far as the Surrey Iron Railway, "Tramway Path" exists for about 400 yards beside the now-Tramlink route in Mitcham.)

'The photo of Waddon Marsh Halt on p26 shows a Wimbledon-bound service arriving. The signalman has the "large" staff in hand to permit entry to the single line section to Mitcham Junction. In return he will receive a 'small' staff for the section from West Croydon, an infallible way of ensuring distinction between the two. The Halt itself dates from July 1930, a contrast to Beddington Lane Halt which opened with the line as plain Beddington on 22 October 1855. The picture on p27, and in particular the splendid bracket signal under which the train is passing, gives an immediate clue to the basic track layout onward to Waddon Marsh, with lines for goods traffic and access to many sidings on both sides of the route.

'Coach No 1 was the vehicle exhibited at various London termini in 1935 to publicise the start of the service (for photographs from the BBC Hulton Picture Library see page 74 of *Southern Reflections* by R. C. Riley and Nigel Harris, Silver Link Publications, 1988) and was clearly located at a number of different stations before settling at Combpyne after Nationalisation and before withdrawal at the end of the 1953 season.'

'The only other piece of double track lay between Wimbledon and Merton Park: the line from Merton Abbey and Tooting made a junction here. The Tooting line lost its passenger services in March 1929, the junction at Tooting being severed then. Double throughout until the Up line went out of use in November 1935, much of the branch was retained for goods traffic until closure in May 1972. Among the businesses using it were Lines Brothers, the manufacturers of Triang toys.

'By the way, the 4SUB at the down platform at West Croydon

Graham Bowring has kindly sent this view to Mike King recently, with grateful thanks to both for permission to use the image and a very informative caption. Quoting Graham, 'The photograph, a scan from an old postcard given to my wife many years ago, shows her father, seated (about 16) with his mother and sister, on holiday in SR Camping Coach No 1 at Port Isaac Road in, we think, 1938. When this family photo was taken they will have had no idea of its significance to those of us interested in SR rolling stock some 80 years later.

(p32) displays the "06" headcode signifying a longstanding "rounder" which, in this direction, started at Victoria. It had reached this point *via* Crystal Palace and Norwood Junction to continue through Sutton, Wimbledon, Tooting, Streatham, Herne Hill and Blackfriars to Holborn Viaduct. In the up direction there were occasions when the train lay over for up to 20 minutes at West Croydon, occupying the (not visible) bay to the left of the platform building seen beyond the "WIM". It's odd how the everyday and mundane of those times now, looking back, arouses such nostalgia. Even the old pre-Bulleid 4SUBs had "something" about them totally absent in today's EMUS. As to the 2BIL and 4LAV (p28/29), did any other stock come near them for comfort? Contrast the former with Bulleid's 2HAL … !'

Finally, for this issue a piece from Chris Sayers-Leavy: 'Just basic observations/comments really – but these are directly quotable as matters arising from SW37.

'The sketch at the bottom of page 46. No direct info here, but I would suggest that the simple matter is that there is no security at all in the manufacturer's "pin & eye" coupling. With no suspension, these trolleys could be quite lively on the track creating the risk that the manufacturer's coupling might shake apart unexpectedly … and there are no failsafe brakes on these units.

'The trolleys pictured at the top of page 40 and bottom of page 47 seem to be of the 17A type whilst that at the bottom of page 40 looks to be a type 27. The trailer appears to be a bit of a home-made affair, at least it is not made by Wickham from what I can see as it is of a much more substantial form of construction than the normal Wickham products.

'The picture on page 36 shows the basic Wickham trolley turntable that was still being used into the early 1980s. After

a couple of accidents with the Southern's heavier diesel-powered 27 trolleys, their use was banned by the HMRI and as this also meant that they could not be "turned" out on the track, so they could not comply with the rule book either, and after being caught out a few times being driven backwards at speed – with the operator facing forwards – they rapidly went out of use. The other factors in their demise was the need for a third-rail isolation – the now necessary isolation earthing arrangements required – and finally and by no means least – because the using department did not want to pay for having them maintained!

'The "flying banana" picture on p94. These vehicles were certainly quite light compared to the SR EMUs in terms of axle loadings. Re the operation of track circuits, did the GWR use the same Track Circuit equipment as the SR? As I understand it, the SR used AC track circuits – to ensure immunisation from DC traction currents? The GWR would not have had the same problem, were their track circuits perhaps DC? Just a thought. The vehicle does not appear to be ATC fitted – which could have been another GWR explanation.

'Finally the picture on page 90 re smoke deflectors. Just compare the gaps between the smoke deflectors and the boiler on both of the engines shown and it is hardly surprising to see how ineffective the Bulleid ones were, plus check out the driver's line of sight. By trying to solve one problem it likely made another one worse.

'The end of steam working on the Isle of Wight was a delightful piece, more please as I have fond memories of holidays spent on the Island and visits there in 1965/6 before the steam services finished and some of the lines closed.' (*We will do what we can – Ed.*)

The last letter in this issue's 'Rebuilt' makes a positive comment about our recent photo feature on the end of steam on the Isle of Wight. How then could I refuse a request for more? Hence here is a recent find by Frank Abraham of No 35 *Freshwater* entering Ventnor, probably around 1966.

Fifty Years On
Counting Down to July 2017
Part Four – Summer 1967
The Photographs of Jim Seddon by Andrea Durrant

In this final part recalling the months, weeks and days leading up to 9 July 1967, I suspect several readers will have their very own recollections of the period in question. I can only recount what others have already said elsewhere: we were unwilling to accept it would – could – ever happen. Steam had been a part of our lives, every time we travelled (certainly on the South Western main line), green coaches, green(ish) engines. The 'ish' was the grime that often obliterated the colour underneath but it was still steam and there was a 'presence', a symbolism of speed and power, certainly from the Pacific types. Of course, such was an amateur's perspective. I was not the one who had to crawl underneath, not lift the shovel for miles on end and not coax a poorly performing machine to keep to a timetable.

Class 4MT No 75074 is serviced at Nine Elms motive power depot. This was one of the engines that lasted until the end although whether, as Jim suggests later, there was any real seriousness in suggesting some of the Standard types might be transferred away for further service is open to doubt. Possibly the way steam types had been allowed to run down was the governing factor. In the end No 75074 remained in one piece only until the autumn of 1967, being dismembered at a scrapyard in Norfolk.

I was a daily traveller up the end of July 1967 and yet, because of the ever increasingly run-down appearance of steam, I regret now that I failed to take much notice in those last weeks. Instead it was a strange quietness that seemed to descend on that first Monday of the full electric service with mutterings from the passengers on the platforms as to what the service would be like. In the end it was almost a sort of anti-climax: calm, efficient but something was missing. We got used to it in the end, although it did seem strange to pass Eastleigh shed with its tracks devoid of engines and by the time of the return later that day already in the first throws of demolition. I recall lying in bed that evening and listening to a strange sort of quiet, the sound of a steam engine working hard up the climb through Winchester was missing. Before, it would be a sound that would arrive and disappear corresponding to whether the train was inside one of the cuttings or on an embankment. Funny things we recall. That was one, the other was more akin to the inner man: no more the smell of frying bacon from the restaurant car on the various morning trains to London, one in particular, officially the 'Royal Wessex', but to us the 'egg and bacon'. The service may have become more efficient but for a number of passengers I know the 'aroma' of steam had gone.

On 18 June 1967, the RCTS organised a 'Farewell to Steam' tour in aid of the Southern Railwaymen's home for children (Woking Homes). Starting from Waterloo, the route was via Guildford, Fareham, Southampton, Bournemouth and Weymouth with the return from Weymouth via Eastleigh and Salisbury. Two engines were used, Class 5MT No 73029 and 'West Country' No 34023 *Blackmore Vale*. The pair are seen approaching Vauxhall on the Windsor lines.

On Saturday 10 June 1967, No 34013, formerly carrying the name *Okehampton*, in charge of the 7.23am Bournemouth to Waterloo is about to pass through Byfleet and New Haw.

On the same day, Jim recorded No 35023 (formerly *Holland-Afrika Line*) at the same location but this time heading south west towards Bournemouth with the 9.24am holiday special. At the time No 35023 was reported as being much used as it was very free steaming but against this it was a rough ride. No 35023 had the distinction of taking the last rostered steam turn from Waterloo, the 9.30am Bournemouth and Weymouth. It returned to Nine Elms later the same day and was kept in steam as a stand-by on Sunday 9 July but was destined never to run again under its own power.

Opposite top: One of the final steam workings to and from Salisbury which retained steam for the morning and late evening commuter trains until the end. 'Class 5' No 73093, leaking steam somewhat, is seen on the approach to Wimbledon, London bound with the 6.49am up train on Friday 8 July.

Bottom: The Waterloo–Basingstoke commuter workings also retained steam on some services until the end. No 34018 (formerly *Axminster*) in charge of one such train west of Wimbledon on 16 June.

Super power for the 6.49am Salisbury–Waterloo service on 28 June, No 35023 was recorded approaching Woking with two non-corridor suburban coaches coupled immediately behind the tender.

No 34089 (formerly *602 Squadron*) arriving at Woking with the same train two days later. The bowler-hat brigade amongst the usual early morning crown will be noted, some no doubt upset if anyone dared to sit in 'their' seat. The engine is clean, having been used on rail tour duty 12 days earlier.

As No 34089 moves off, No 35003 (formerly *Royal Mail*) comes blasting past on the main with the 8.10am down. We may hope the steam from the driver's side of the cab is only because the injector feed has just been turned on.

Likely one of the final boat trains to carry a headboard. The 9.20am 'Springbok' boat train (Union Castle Line) special to Southampton. The service was 9.20am from Waterloo worked by No 34060 (formerly *25 Squadron*), which would arrive in plenty of time for the sailing of the *Pendennis Castle* later in the day.

Jim reports this as the 'unusual sight of Nos 73118 (formerly *King Leodegrance*) and 73092 heading towards Waterloo'. We are not told when nor, unfortunately, the circumstances.

Below and opposite page: In June 1967 BR announced that five special trains would run on Saturday 2 July as a 'Farewell to Steam' commemoration. In the event just two ran and neither of these was filled to capacity as the Southern Region elected to charge participants twice the normal fare – and it was normal stock, not Pullman. The engines selected for the two trains were No 35008 *Orient Line* and No 35028 *Clan Line*, contemporary reports stating that both engines would have their nameplates restored for the occasion. They are seen here at Nine Elms prior to the workings, both having received the attention of the cleaners – more like whatever staff could be found by this time.

No 34025 (formerly *Whimple*) on the ash pit at Nine Elms on 8 July having brought in the 8.42am Bournemouth to Waterloo. The engine would have one more turn yet, in charge of the 9.35 Waterloo to Bournemouth on the final day of steam operation.

With the attention so far concentrated on the main line workings and Nine Elms itself, we should not forget that empty stock workings between Waterloo and Clapham Junction were still taking place. These were mainly now in the hands of the Ivatt and BR standard tank engines. No 82019 – the last of its class – was snapped from a passing train at Clapham Junction with just six days of steam working left to go.

At Nine Elms the turntable was situated in the extreme south west corner of the yard beyond the ash pit. Engines such as No 34037 (formerly *Clovelly*) seen here, would come on to the turntable and be turned to face the shed. They would depart in similar fashion in order to be ready to leave and run tender first back to Waterloo. Coal and water would be taken before leaving.

The final weekend, when there seemed to be more visitors than railwaymen.

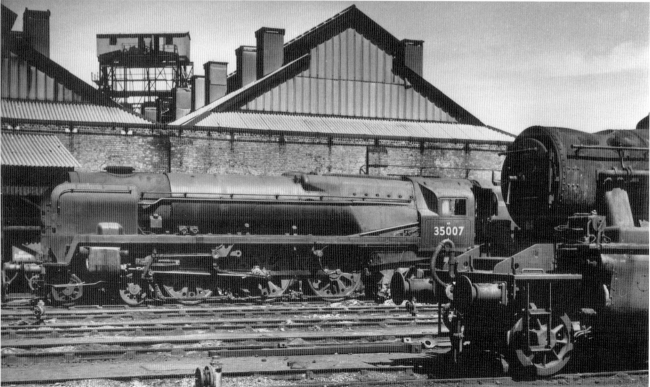

Right: One of those in steam – No 41298.

Opposite top: Sunday 9 July was a day of brilliant sunshine. Nos 73022 and 34057 (formerly *Biggin Hill*) have just one more duty to be performed for their owners – as so much scrap. This is of course very similar to the well known David Shepherd painting.

Bottom: On that same July afternoon Jim counted 26 engines at Nine Elms. Three were in steam, Nos 41298, 75075 and 35023. Others out of steam (including those already withdrawn) were Nos 41284/319, 80012/35/140, 73022/37/119, 76064, 35007/8/12/28, 34001/2/13/15/18/19/23/34/100 and 34057/88. In this view No 41284, minus its chimney, reposes quietly with No 35007 behind.

Below and spread overleaf: During the afternoon turn of duty No 75075 was deemed not required, the fire was dropped and the engine then backed into the shed for last time.

On 10 July all the Bulleid Pacifics were officially withdrawn. Jim comments that some of the Standard types were held back for possible transfer to other regions but, as we know, this did not happen. A few staff were retained to empty boilers and tenders of water and remove coal from the tenders, an operation that would last for some weeks. After that the engines would slowly move in melancholy procession to Salisbury pending sale and scrap. Nine Elms would become even more of a waste ground, the ghosts of the past now its remaining residents. The site would be developed as the 'new' Covent Garden Market after 1969.

Recollections of a Brighton Apprenticeship 60-plus Years Ago

Adrian Westbury

Holmwood station, the 'home station' of Adrian Westbury. The relevance of this image relative to this article will be found in 'Rebuilt …'
Crecy Transport Heritage Library/LGRP/NRM

In the summer of 1952, and much to the disgust of my headmaster, I left Dorking Grammar School to take up an apprenticeship at Brighton Locomotive Works. I had been offered this following an interview with the Assistant to the Works Manager and having passed the required medical.

Thus on a Monday morning in August of that year I joined the crowd of workmen making their way up New England Road from Preston Circus turning into New England Street and then up the concrete steps to one of the Works entrances. Arriving there, I was directed to the Apprentice Training School, commonly known as the cage.

It was an appropriate name as it was an enclosed compound in the corner of the light plating shop and adjacent to the Millwrights shop. It consisted of a wooden fence about five feet high topped by another two feet of wire mesh, all the woodwork being painted green. The entrance was through a door toward the end of one of the long sides. On the right as you entered was a full-length workbench accessible from both sides and this was repeated on the opposite side. Across the top end was a desk and cupboards for our instructor Mr Nunn and at the opposite end adjacent to the entrance door a medium-size centre lathe and a pillar drilling machine.

When I commenced my training around eight more lads started including Brian Potts, who had two articles on Brighton Works published in early issues of *Southern Way*. A few of us that lived some distance from Brighton had to go into lodgings and I will return to that topic later.

The purpose of the training school was to teach us to use hand tools by working our way through a number of projects. This ensured that we mastered the use of files, saws, chisels, etc. and at the same time we actually made a number of tools that would be of use in our careers such as calipers, engineers square, tool clamps, straight edge, etc. Some of those tools I still have. Also, basic turning on the lathe was undertaken. The training programme stated a period of six months in the school but in practice a group of us were moved out to the fitting shop soon after five months. I think one of the reasons was that with further apprentices starting, the school was becoming

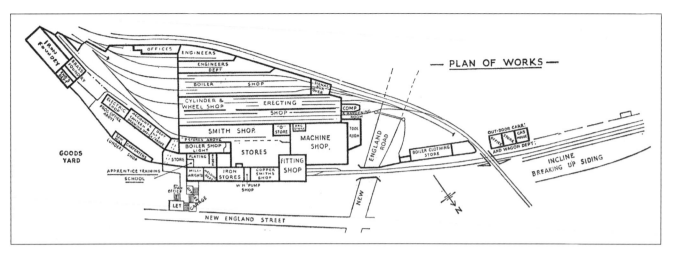

— PLAN OF WORKS —

With apologies for a repeat of this view seen a few years ago in SW, but appropriate as a reminder of the layout of the shops.

overcrowded.

We were also all enrolled at the local Technical Institute for academic studies, initially aimed at securing an ONC (ordinary national certificate) and then progressing to HNC for those capable of going upwards and onwards to membership of professional institutes. I was destined only to make it to ONC level.

Our instructor Mr Nunn was a very patient and calm individual; indeed, I cannot recall him ever losing his temper with any of us even though we must have tried him sorely at times. As was to be expected with a bunch of teenagers, from time to time we got up to various bits of mischief; two of these I recall now. One afternoon we were throwing a handful of dirty cotton waste at each other and eventually the targeted person ducked with the missile carrying on until it came to a stop hitting the instructor – who was sat at his desk – square on the side of the face. He made no comment but just looked long and hard at everyone – end of that episode. The other occasion had more serious consequences and we all received a right good rollicking for it. One lunch time we were lounging around, some reading newspapers, others playing cards, when a gang of young lads from the Boiler Shop appeared and commenced lobbing missiles at us, some of these being brown paper bags full of water and of course we retaliated by throwing anything to hand back at them. More by luck than judgement one of these efforts hit a paper bag and the contents fell on a large piece of metal the men in the light plating shop had been marking out with chalk during the morning. Of course the water washed away their work. Quite an interesting afternoon followed; we never had visits from the boiler shop lads again.

Fitting Shop

In January 1953, along with several others I was moved from the training school to the fitting shop to continue my training. There were five gangs in the fitting shop, each ranging from just four persons to around a dozen. Each gang undertook specific jobs relative to the repair of locos in the erecting shop, we apprentices moving around the various gangs from time to time to increase our knowledge. The first one I was attached to was

Mr Coney's, which dealt with brake gear and axle boxes plus a few other items. Mr Coney, like most chargehands, had a wealth of experience and was getting toward retirement age. During his initial chat with me he asked when my birthday was. I responded with 18 June, to which he then asked, 'What great historical event took place on that date?' I was able to reply that it was the battle of Waterloo in 1815 which seemed to satisfy his curiosity. I subsequently found out his hobby was researching history, so it had got me off to a good start with him. He put me to work with 'Big Dave', who dealt with reconditioning brake gear. Now, when brake gear had been dismantled from locos coming in for repair, it was put through a fire to burn off all the muck and grease. This was very satisfactory, although the down side was that it left a residue of flocking (powdered) rust which transferred itself to hands and overalls. Put on clean overalls on a Monday morning and by the time of the mid morning tea break one was covered with this. The prime objective, though, was to get the components – pull rods cross beams, etc – back to their original specification, which involved removing the worn bushes and fitting new ones, plus, where there was wear in the bush holes or on the cross-shaft spigots, to send these items first to the welding shop to be built up and then on to the machine shop for return to size. There was a small hydraulic press in the shop which we used to press out old bushes and insert new ones. On completion of a set of rods and beams, they were returned to the erecting shop ready for installation on the loco from which they had been removed.

After some weeks with 'Big Dave', Mr Coney moved me on to work on axle boxes. Two fitters undertook this work, with the axle boxes, after removal from the axles in the erecting shop, going through the bosh (a caustic bath) to clean them – at least they emerged relatively clean compared to the brake gear. The procedure was then to remove the worn bearing by prising the 'arms' of the axle box casting apart to release it, then to remove the side liners that rubbed up and down the horn guides. These were held in position on the axle box casting by copper studs that had to be drilled out and new bronze liners fitted, which involved screwing in the studs and then riveting them over. This latter operation was quite amusing to watch with two people taking it in turns to strike the copper and well and truly secure the liner to the casting. The actual bearing comes partially machined but had to be hand finished to fit into the casting.

It was whilst carrying out this job on an axle box for an 'E4' tank that I came to grief. The bearing was partially in the casting but then fell out and in doing so severed the tip of my middle finger on the right hand. Blood everywhere. The fitter told me to put my right arm over my left shoulder and then we ran through the shops to the first aid room, I think many workmen paused to look and wonder why a fitter was chasing an apprentice. The first aid nurse patched me up and gave a pass-out to give the gatekeeper and sent me to hospital. Strange as it may seem nowadays, there was no ambulance and instead I had to go to the front of Brighton station to catch the appropriately numbered bus to the hospital. Once on the bus another problem arose, the nurse had strapped my arm across me so that I could not get at my right-hand trouser pocket to find the money for the bus fare, so, much to the amusement of other passengers, the conductor had to fish through my overalls into my pocket to extract the fare. On returning to the Works and going to the first aid room an older retired man who helped out there was given the job of escorting me to my lodgings to pick up my bits and pieces and then accompany me on the train from Brighton to home. What amused me was he asked the nurse for a bottle of smelling salts, I don't know if they were for him or me. I was to be off work for six weeks whilst the wound healed and, as it was my right hand, I was unable to do much. The family dog had more walks than ever before or afterwards.

When I returned to work, there had been a move around of apprentices and I was now in Mr Wood's gang, which proved to be the most boring and miserable time of my whole apprenticeship. The gang only consisted of Mr Wood and three workmen and at that time all the jobs were fettling new motion parts for the '80xxx' tanks being erected at Brighton. All the valve gear came from the machine shop in a 'raw' state, that is every edge was razor sharp, and our task was to file a radius on all edges and then draw file the rods; most of my time involved carrying this out on union links and combination levers. As if the work was not boring enough, there was a long-standing feud between the three workmen, the two one side of the bench never spoke to the one on the opposite side and if I spoke to them the other one would not speak to me for several days. Conversely, if I spoke to the single one the others just gave me filthy looks. Oh, how I longed for the weekly day at Technical College during that time!

Eventually the next move around came and I went to the gang repairing and reconditioning the smaller brass components. I seemed to get either cylinder drain cocks or gauge glass valves to work on. The procedure was to strip the valve, give it a good wire brushing and then apply grinding paste to the moving parts and, with a semi-rotary motion, bed the male and female faces together. When the surfaces looked smooth and even, the valve was reassembled and asbestos packing tamped down on to the valve top. The actual asbestos was held in trays along the bench and one just took a handful and rammed it home. To test it, the valve was coated in soapy water again from dishes along the bench and coupled to a compressed air line to check if it was sound or giving off bubbles; if the latter, it was stripped down again and subjected to more grinding. When it appeared OK, the chargehand would himself check it and pass it. It was a friendly gang and time passed quickly. The next move was to the erecting shop which took place on 1 January 1954.

'K' class 2-6-0 No 32339 on one of the shed lines at Brighton. Part of the Works and offices may be seen as the tall buildings in the background.

Erecting Shop

Like the fitting shop, the erecting shop was made up of gangs of workmen each under the supervision of a chargehand. Time has dulled my memory as to how many gangs there were but it must have been around seven or eight. I was placed in Mr Woodhead's gang and put to work with two men. One, an older man, had seen service in World War 1, whilst the other was not long out of his time as an apprentice. I cannot say either inspired me, for they showed no real interest in the jobs we were given. However, we worked on a number of locos and I give details below. One incident stands out in my memory and, had I not seen, I would have thought it a bit of fiction. On that particular afternoon I noticed the older man was not around, so asked the younger one where he was. The reply was 'Gone to the races' – and indeed he had. I discovered he had crossed over to the running shed, obviously removed his overalls and hidden them somewhere, and then walked out of the shed unnoticed by the coming and going of loco men into New England Road, catching a trolleybus to Race Hill. Then, after a couple of hours or so, he retraced his way back in time for knocking off. (I do not recall if he was smiling upon his return.) After a few weeks, Mr Woodhead teamed me up with a different mate, a man in his early thirties and a joy to work with. This time I was taught a lot, my new mate always keen to get on with the job and explain everything to me.

As in the fitting shop, there was very little heating and only basic provision for washing at the end of the morning or afternoon. Towards knocking-off time, a labourer would set up a bucket of water on a baulk of timber, then go to the smiths shop with a lump of metal and long handled tongs, heat the metal till it glowed red and then return and plunge it into the bucket. Anything up to a dozen men would then try to dip into it and clean the worst of the muck off before clocking off. One problem at Brighton was that there was always a struggle to find a cupboard under the benches to keep one's tools and other items. I eventually found one in the west bay near the north end, albeit some distance from where we worked in Woodhead's gang. At least I had somewhere secure to keep things. It was interesting that the next cupboard was occupied by an older apprentice, who had set himself a hobby target to visit and see a match at every English and Welsh league football club. I remember one Monday morning he told me he had been to Carlisle on the Saturday, probably the furthest ground from Brighton.

One job that I remember working on with my good mate was on No 10001, the ex-LMS main line diesel. At that time all four main line diesels were working on the Southern Region out of Waterloo on West of England and Bournemouth line duties, whilst at the same time the third Southern one, No 10203, was being built at Brighton. The diesels were frequent visitors to the Works and the English Electric Company had their technicians there to carry out specialist repairs whilst we British Railways staff did the mundane work. In this instance we had to bleed the engine fuel system so that the engine could be fired up. The Works shunter, the little 'A1X', pulled 10001 out of the shop on what was a bitterly cold day. By the time we had completed the job, what with the cold weather and cold diesel fuel flowing over our hands, we were well and truly frozen so that when the engine was started up, despite the noise, we stayed in the engine room to thaw out.

Brighton steam shed with its usual, for the time, plethora of engines present. This was the exit route to the Brighton Races for the man referred to whilst Adrian was spending time in the Erecting Shop.

On 21 June I was moved to Mr Whitehouse's gang but, before giving details of that time, here is a list of locos worked on up to that period:

No 32529, Class C2X 'intermediate'.
No 30053, Class M7 'intermediate'
No 32506, Class E4 'wheels and boxes'
No 80019, Class 4 'light casual'
No 32346, Class K 'light casual'
No 10001, Main line Diesel 'light casual'
No 42069, Class 4MT 'blower pipe'
No 42100, Class 4MT 'wheels and boxes'
No 34110, Class BB (66 Squadron) 'light casual'
No 10001, Main line Diesel 'light casual'
No 30929, Class V, 'general'

Mr Whitehouse teamed me up with another good mate also in his early thirties and also one who relished getting stuck into the job in hand. Whilst with him we undertook work on 10 different locos, including several general repairs which I found particularly interesting, these requiring such a wide variety of jobs to be carried out.

Most of the locos we worked on were in the West Bay of the erecting shop which was more cramped than the East Bay and so everywhere always looked jumbled up and the supposed clear walk way between the two rows of locos was only clear about once a year for the annual open day. On the actual open day, when for a small donation the public was guided round the various shops, we apprentices were given the job of acting as guides to each group of around 10 people. It made for an interesting change despite the somewhat ribald comments when you took the group past your current workmates.

One of the locos in for a general repair that we worked on was the Brighton Atlantic *South Foreland* (No 32421) and two published photos of it during that time are known. One by Brian Morrison has appeared in several publications and is a three-quarter view with the boiler in position and painted but still awaiting wheeling; the other appears in the Oakwood Press bibliography of Ron Jarvis and shows me in the cab.

Obviously, from time to time there were incidents that remain in the memory and one of these was when we were in the pit under No 30905 (*Tonbridge*) removing one of the spring hanger brackets. I was holding the drift (the round punch) by means of some welding wire wrapped round it and my mate was striking it with a heavy hammer to drive out the rivets. One aim at the drift just caught it a glancing blow and the hammer swung round and caught me square on the forehead and I went down completely knocked out. When I came round all I could see were anxious faces peering at me and I am told that my first words were 'have I missed pay time?' as it was a Friday morning coming up to lunch time when we received our weekly pay.

The full list of locos worked on during my time in Mr Whitehead's gang, which ended on 8 November 1954, was:

No 30285, Class T9 'smoke box'
No 32329, Class N15X (*Stephenson*) 'general'
No 10202, Main line Diesel 'casual'
No 30133, Class M7 'smoke box'
No 32492, Class E4 'intermediate'
No 32421, Class H2 'general'

No 10001, Main line Diesel 'casual'
No 30905, Class V (*Tonbridge*)'intermediate'
No 30712, Class T9 'general'
No 34070, Class BB (*Manston*) 'wheels and boxes'.

Before leaving the erecting shop, I relate an amusing incident that took place one morning. The latrines were situated outside the north end of the shop and consisted of an open pipe with a constant flow of water covered by a series of cubicles. Every morning certain workmen would make their way there about 10am taking the *Racing Post* with them and sit trying to find the winners of the day's races. These they would then scribble down and pass to the strictly illegal bookies runner. On this particular day a couple of apprentices decided to have some fun and entered the first cubicle with some paper and oil-soaked cotton waste. Having first set light to it, they floated it on to the running water. Exit each cubicle, the door flew open and the occupant emerged with overalls and trousers around their ankles and shouting unprintable oaths! I think the chargehands and foremen had a sly laugh at all this.

Machine Shop

Moving to the machine shop was quite a shock after the hurly burly of the erecting shop. We apprentices were in a small gang with our own chargehand, Mr Andrews, always known as 'Ginger'. There were four or five of us at any one time in this gang, each working on a centre lathe. Most of the work was fairly basic turning and screw cutting with Ginger keeping our noses to the grindstone. Unfortunately, he had a personal problem in that he suffered with smelly feet; hence we always knew when he was standing behind as you operated the lathe. Ginger was another great one for horse racing and being situated on the far side of the machine shop by the windows, he always had his binoculars at the ready when there was a meeting at Brighton racecourse.

I recall one occasion involving the smokebox door of an '80xxx' series tank. This involved holding the casting in a four-jaw chuck and turning and then screw cutting the spigot that passed through the smoke box front and was nutted from behind. I had successfully completed a number of these when my concentration obviously slipped and I did not disengage the lead screw quick enough with the result the tool bit into the casting and was forced out of the chuck, Ginger was not best pleased but we managed to salvage it. I must have eventually redeemed myself in his eyes, because one day I was given a special job which entailed cutting a 'V' groove into eight bronze castings that were to be installed into the sliding doors between the cabs and the interior of No 10203. The tool room had supplied a special jig to hold these, so that was my contribution to the construction of No 10203.

It became very hot in that shop as the summer wore on and we were in the habit of removing our shirts and wearing just our boiler suit overall. One afternoon the chap on the lathe in front of me had left his overall open and was making some quite heavy cuts on the job in hand when a piece of red hot swarf landed on the hairs of his chest; we were witness to quite a lively dance! I don't think I was cut out to be turner. I much preferred the erecting shop life.

Class 4MT No 80144, built at Brighton in September 1956 – might this be one of the engines for which Adrian was responsible for the smokebox door? It would have a life of just less than 10 years, being withdrawn from Nine Elms in 1966.

Lodgings

I wrote above about going into lodgings, for as my home was between Horsham and Dorking it was simply not feasible to travel daily to Brighton, although I did return home at weekends. There was a lady in one of the offices who, as part of her work, sorted out lodgings for apprentices that needed them. She found me a place with a family a trolley bus ride out of Brighton towards Hollinbury. The husband worked in accounts at the Works, whilst the daughter was a tracer in the drawing office and the daughter's boyfriend also worked in the drawing office. I was quite happy there and seemed settled; that is, until I started work in the Fitting Shop on brake gear and went back after work filthy dirty compared to the clean state the others were in. The lady of the house took exception to this and her husband was prevailed upon to get me moved.

I was found alternative lodgings just off Preston Circus, which at least saved me the trolleybus fares each day. Already there were Max and Tony, two apprentices who had commenced their training at New Year 1953, plus another older lad, who was an apprentice at Feltham MPD but, like all apprentices at MPDs, had to serve one year of his training at a main works. We all got on well together and it was whilst I was here that I had my accident and had to go off sick. Unfortunately, upon my return to work, things had changed at the lodgings and not for the better. The landlady was now taking in summer visitors and so we apprentices were barred from using the bathroom and had to wash in the kitchen sink but we could not do so when returning from work and instead had to wait until she had cleared away and washed up after the evening meal. Max and Tony had already left, having found themselves a self-catering apartment in the Seven Dials area of Brighton. Having visited them, I decided to get something similar and an advertisement in the *Brighton Evening Argus* produced five replies. The second one I viewed suited me fine; it was on a road between London Road station and Preston Park, the couple who lived there were retired and had one room fitted out as being self contained with a bed, wardrobe, table, cupboards, wash basin and small electric cooker, all that I needed. I spent just over two years there, arriving on Monday

evenings and leaving on Friday mornings. Whilst at home over the weekend, my mother would make up the necessary ingredients for four breakfasts and four evening meals whilst I had a midday lunch in the Works canteen. Mr and Mrs Walker were a lovely couple; he was a former marine engineer and sometimes of an evening would invite me to join them in their lounge for a chat on engineering topics. They also introduced me to the delights of single malt whisky.

Leaving Brighton

Ever since I commenced work, there had been rumours from time to time that Brighton Works was to close, although it was 1958 before that happened. We apprentices were told unofficially that we would not be made redundant but moved to either Ashford or Eastleigh to complete our training, I didn't fancy either place, wondering what sort of reception we would get as it appeared that not a lot of love existed between the three Works. During my time in the erecting shop, the senior foreman also retired and in his place was appointed Mr Ernie Broome, who had transferred from Stafford Road Works in Wolverhampton. He was not overjoyed at this move and quite frequently returned home to Wolverhampton at weekends. I cannot now remember how I came to talk with him but when he learnt I originated from the West Midlands he seemed to keep an eye on me. So, whilst in the Machine Shop and with rumours rife again, I sought out Mr Broome for advice. He suggested I transfer to a MPD to complete my training and said 'leave it with me'. A few weeks later on a Monday morning I saw him come across the Machine Shop and have a few words with 'Ginger', our chargehand. He then came to me and said, 'Next Saturday morning, interview at 11.00 with the Shed master at Stourbridge MPD', emphasising his next two words, 'BE THERE'. I duly presented myself on the Saturday morning and was accepted for a transfer. On the following Monday morning I went to see Mr Broome to thank him and tell him the outcome. As this was in July, it was arranged that I would finish at Brighton when the Works closed for the annual holiday in August. What followed was time with the Western Region and I was able to complete my apprenticeship in 1957.

What's In a Picture?

Nigel Barnes-Evans aka 'Baffled of Boscombe'

It is sometimes amazing what a little digging can achieve from just one image. I use the attached as an example: one photograph found in a drawer and yet with some detective work it was able to tell a detailed story.

A quick glance and it appears to be just another 'Standard 5', No 73088, on a train at the now closed station of Boscombe near Bournemouth. Immediate comments are that the station opened in 1897 and closed in October 1965 and during its life was the most convenient stopping place for Dean Park, home of the Bournemouth and Boscombe Athletic FC. The view was taken on 16 February 1957; No 73088 was then less than 18 months old, having been built at Derby in September 1955 and at the time allocated to Stewarts Lane. It was then also un-named, although in 1959 it would be given the name 'Joyous Gard', which title had previously adorned 'King Arthur' No 30741.

But it was the coaching stock that really puzzled me. Why would a Southern based engine be hauling LNER stock; almost certainly it was a special working, but from where and likewise to where?

Fortunately, we have a date, 16 February 1957, the occasion of the 5th round tie of the FA cup in which Bournemouth & Boscombe Athletic (sic) were to play Tottenham Hotspur at Dean Park. To cope with the anticipated level of support from the away team, at least four special trains were run, two from Waterloo and two from South Tottenham. It is one of the specials from South Tottenham that is depicted here.

Dealing first, though, with the trains from Waterloo, these were scheduled to leave at 10.45 and 11.05am respectively, stopping en route only at Southampton for water before calling at Boscombe, and then Bournemouth Central. It is possible some of the train's occupants may have deliberately alighted at the latter stop – partners of supporters, etc. Working ecs, the stock was then taken on to Bournemouth West for stabling. Each consisted of eight passenger vehicles including a restaurant/buffet. In the down direction from Waterloo the *Railway Observer* for March 1957 (p74) advises the engines used from Waterloo were Nos 34011(*Tavistock*) and 34065 (*Hurricane*) respectively. The weekly Special Traffic Notice giving details of the workings (and also that involving No 73088 as will be described later) does not mention what happened to the engines after the stock had been berthed at Boscombe but there are two possibilities. Either they returned to Bournemouth Central shed or they were turned on the triangle at Branksome and serviced at the small depot there to await departure time. It should also be mentioned that, whilst we are assuming these same two engines were used for the return runs, that is not confirmed. Neither is it confirmed if a third 'if required' special ran from Waterloo. If so, this would have left at 11.20am. Had only a limited number of passengers arrived for this train and/or the earlier two trains were full – and we do not know the loadings – then any stragglers may well have been directed to an ordinary service train. Finally, it is worth mentioning that the two services known to have operated varied in their respective schedules by a few minutes, despite having similar weight trains. This was simply to allow for them to fit in with existing services and therefore line occupancy.

So, having dealt with the trains from Waterloo, let us now turn to the special trains from South Tottenham. These left at 8.40 and 8.52am, both formed of Eastern Region stock with each including a buffet. In the down direction, an ER loco took the trains as far as Kensington Olympia, where Nos 73088 – for the first train – and sister engine No 73089 – for the second – were attached. Both the Class 5's were Stewarts Lane engines, with the suggestion that it was likely Stewarts Lane rather than Nine Elms engines were used as the former had easier access to Kensington. (Another possibility is that Nine Elms did not have spare motive power and it was easier and certainly cheaper to allocate the engines from Stewarts Lane rather than bring up light engines from elsewhere. It is very likely Nine Elms crews would have been used for the simple reason of route knowledge.) From here the trains were routed via Clapham Junction (5-minute and 1-minute stops respectively) and thence through East Putney to join the main line at Byfleet and New Haw. Again there was a water stop at Southampton Central but otherwise the same comments as those applied to the Waterloo trains regarding times and also specified lines ('LL' – local line or 'TL' – through line) being reported at intervals. Once more there was also provision for a third special if required and again we have no information whether this ran. The trains also deposited at Boscombe and Bournemouth Central before also running ecs to Bournemouth West – the carriage sidings would have been busy on that day! Earlier comments regarding the disposal of the engines off the Waterloo trains again apply.

It is interesting to consider for the moment the potential operating difficulties associated with the running of these extra 'if required' services. Practically there is simply no way that a train could be made ready at a few moments or even a couple of hours' notice and so it is more like the Weekly Notice when it was prepared made provision with the final decision notified on a Special Notice. Whilst we have access to the WN we do not have any SN.

Having dealt with the movement of fans to the area, with soccer or spending the order of the day, how about the match itself? Well Bournemouth won 3-1 but Tottenham fans might have taken solace that Bournemouth was beaten in the next round, again at home, 1-2, by Manchester United. In the photograph, what is believed to have been the first Tottenham train – 8.40am departure from South Tottenham; 12.15 to 12.19pm arrival at Boscombe – is seen in the process of slowing to a stop to let the travelling fans off for the short walk to Dean Court football ground, hence the staff visible in picture. What we do not know is how any of the trains actually ran on the day.

The return specials left Bournemouth West at 4.40pm (destination Waterloo), 4.58pm (destination South Tottenham), 5.10pm (destination Waterloo) and 5.18pm (destination South Tottenham). A feature common to the first three was that all were shown as routed 'TL', meaning through line at Bournemouth Central; it was only the last which stopped to pick up at the latter station. Following all also having collected their quota of disappointed fans at Boscombe, it is unusual to report that each was shown as running non-stop through Southampton, making a water stop at Basingstoke instead. Concerning the return of the South Tottenham trains, the STN shows the Southern engines as working through to South Tottenham, no doubt with a pilot man collected en route, and thence with the ecs on to Stratford. No mention is made of the engines' return to their home territory.

The last two 'if required' services would have departed Bournemouth West at 5.40pm and 5.50pm, the first for Waterloo and the second for South Tottenham. Both of these would have started their collection of passengers at Bournemouth Central and also stopped for water twice each at Southampton Central and Basingstoke. For all the workings the schedules were also far from arduous, 2hr 30min to 2hr 40min the average for the Waterloo trains in either direction.

With thanks to the Bournemouth Railway Club and in particular Graham Hancock who supplied the football information.

Testing the Tank Engines

We recently came across some notes by the late John G. Click appertaining to a Southern Region interchange trial which occurred in 1948 away from the 'glitz and glamour' of the main line but which was also taking place around the same time as the main line locomotive exchanges. This involved a comparative test between an imported London Midland Class 4 Fairburn tank and a Southern 'W' class.

As a prelude to what follows, it should be mentioned that at the time of Nationalisation, the motive power and with it the operating departments of the Southern Region, were defunct in one type of engine – a powerful passenger or mixed traffic tank engine. Partly this stemmed from the Sevenoaks accident of 1927 when a tank engine at the head of an express derailed with much loss of life. After this there was, understandably, a reluctance to pursue the 'big tank engine' design type, notwithstanding all three of the other pre-nationalisation railways were, and had been, operating passenger services with this type of machine very successfully for many years.

So far as the Southern was concerned, their equivalent type of operation – suburban passenger – was nearly all in the hands of electric trains and as such what need existed was generally catered for. But there were still examples of where such need was identified and which was, to quote John Click from elsewhere, 'in the hands of gasping tank engines from the days of the LBSCR and LSWR'. Whilst perfectly capable on branch lines with limited loads and generous schedules, they were of limited use elsewhere.

Enter the frame then Mr Bulleid with all his revolutionary ideas. His 'double-ended tank engine', as it was sometimes referred to (what would eventually emerge as the 'Leader'), was recognised as being unlikely to fit the bill, and is where John Click takes up the story.

'In the spring of 1948, the Southern Motive Power Officers saw clearly the way the "Leader" wind was blowing. Having found their worst fears confirmed, they went to Rudgard[1] at the Kremlin *(meaning Marylebone Road, the Headquarters of BR – Ed)* and came home with a promise of two of the latest LMS 2-6-4 tanks for trial. This loan came at the time of the more famous Interchange Trials, of which I saw nothing, and

[1] *Lt Col Harold Rudgard OBE TD MIME (1884–1958) was Chief Officer (Motive Power) at the nationalised Railway Executive and a former Superintendent of Motive Power on the LMS.*

No 42198 leaving Waterloo with the 10.54am service to Salisbury, probably in April 1948. *Southern Region Magazine*

involved Nos 42198 and 42199[2]. The first one came to Ashford and worked on duties usually allocated to my beloved Wainwright 'J' class 0-6-4 tanks. *(JGC does not elaborate why he had such feeling for the 'J' type.)*

'After local trips confirmed how well they performed, a high-speed trip was arranged from Ashford to Tonbridge and back (26.4 miles) chimney first going up and bunker first coming back, both in a booked time of only 26 minutes start to stop. The load was eight bogies plus the Hallade track recording coach. I begged Harry Attwell[3], who was on the engine, to let me go but to no avail – even in the empty train. Needless to say, both trips went very well, so that when Mr Bulleid heard about them (and one can assume he was not consulted) he recalled the investigations which he took part in on the LNER, following the 1927 Sevenoaks accident, when a two-cylinder 'River' class had derailed due to a combination of track irregularities, lively springing and surging water in her tanks.

'Bulleid remembered that he had a stud of Maunsell's "W" class 2-6-4 tanks that had been built to use parts from the "Rivers" when those locomotives were rebuilt to "U" class 2-6-0s. From the start they had been banned from all passenger work but had long since done excellent work with transfer freights across London.

'Why not run a "W" against the "LM" tanks? He'd start another Interchange Trial of his own, if only to have the satisfaction of showing how wrong Ellson had been not to let him have his 2-8-2: all that fuss about a two-wheeled leading truck!

'The single three-cylinder "River" tank No 890 had run well at high speed between St Neots and Huntingdon and even though the "Ws" only had 5ft 6in wheels, that would be no impediment: he had, after all, changed the rules about piston speed. Phones rang and it was found that No 31918 was just out from a general repair at Ashford, had worked a freight to Dover and back and was thus "run in". "Don't let it go back to its home shed!" There was even a rumour that the "W" would go back into the works to be repainted in malachite green for the occasion. Those in the know should have arranged to increase the oil feed to the inside big end, because it had rightly been pared down to the minimum needed for its slow freight duties. Instead they muttered how foolish such a trial was, did nothing, and wrung their hands, fearing the worst. The result: No 31918 got to Tonbridge all right inside the 26 minutes but the middle big end was, not surprisingly, dangerously hot. Cylinder oil was thrown over it and off she went again bunker first. Attwell told me afterwards that she had bucked and rolled alarmingly at Paddock Wood and again at Headcorn where a sudden walloping from inside signalled that the big end had broken up. After limping in to Ashford the loco came on shed where I met it in. The brasses had disintegrated; chunks were everywhere: it was the hottest bearing I ever saw and a close call. Wagging heads said "I told you so" but I was not one of them. No doubt Rudgard was amused but I considered Bulleid to have been badly let down. However true it had been in Maunsell's time that "dripping water wears away a stone", Bulleid didn't have the time. Strangely, he seems to have put the incident down to "one of those things", for he wasn't one to be vindictive.

The other LMR tank worked the Waterloo to Basingstoke trains very competently so an order to build them for the Southern was issued and Brighton, used to the "8Fs" from the war, got on with them after the "Leader" programme was stopped. The "M7" replacement did arrive in the end.'

---

[2] *Nos 42198/9 were built at Horwich in March and April 1948 respectively. Both are shown as having been allocated to Stirling as their first shed. JGC does not give a date for these tests other than they took place in 'spring', hence it is likely the engines were brand new and arrived straight from the builder. The fact the event was overshadowed by what JGC refers to as the 'Interchange Trials' may also explain why this test has in the main been largely forgotten. The exception is an entry on p129 of* The Locomotive History of the South Eastern & Chatham Railway *by D. L. Bradley published by the RCTS which gives some detail of the same test stated to have taken place in April 1948.*

[3] *Harry Attwell was in charge of the Southern locomotive testing section based at Brighton.*

Sykes Lock and Block and other Southern Instruments

Alan Postlethwaite

Introduction

This article reviews the development of telegraphy and interlocking with particular reference to the Southern companies. It uses short explanations in layman's language. For a full history of telegraphy and more detailed descriptions, I can recommend References 1, 2 and 3 at the end of this piece.

Above: A picture of tidiness and cleanliness at Ryde St Johns Road, this time with SR standard three-position block instruments in use working to Ryde Pierhead and, during the summer season, Smallbrook Junction. In winter months single line token working was the norm, hence the Tyers No 9 instrument on the extreme right.

Right: A plethora of Sykes instruments at Hounslow. The frame with its square nameplates was supplied by Stevens. The lever lead plates at Ryde (next image) are of the long oval type which became standard on the SR (BR Southern Region). (The best way to learn the Lock and Block system is hands-on. The SR established a new signalling school [with model railway] at Clapham Junction in the long elevated corridor from the closed L&SWR booking office in Plough Road. See also pictures of the school which appeared in SW7.)

This actual article was inspired by the memoirs of Charles Anderson. These were published in four parts in SW Issues 32 to 35. The second part (Ref. 4) includes a bold statement that the London & South Western Railway (L&SWR) 'never understood the block system from first to last'. I take that as a challenge for you and me to try to understand it for ourselves, at least in principle, and to identify the Southern people who pioneered signal box devices to improve railway safety.

Time Interval Working

The earliest railways used the Time Interval system of dispatching trains, whereby a policeman showed a flag or lamp to indicate Danger (red), Proceed with Caution (green) or Line Clear (white). This worked well when traffic comprised only a few trains per day. But as traffic volume grew, time intervals were decreased and the system became patently unsafe. Any delayed train could result in collision. It was also inefficient since the line was usually clear long before the second train was released.

The Wheatstone Bridge

This was invented by Samuel Christie in 1833. It was developed for commercial use by William Cooke and Charles Wheatstone and patented in 1843. The diagram shows the principle: powered by battery, current flows around either side of a diamond which has four different resistors. Meter 'V' measures a small voltage across the central joins. Resistor R is variable such that the measured voltage at V can be positive or negative. The needle of 'V' could therefore be made to receive coded messages by clunking or ringing a bell. It could also be made to resemble a signal arm as a visual indication of whether a railway line is clear.

The Telegraph

The first demonstration of the railway telegraph was in 1837 between Euston and Camden Town but the first permanent telegraph opened in 1839 between Paddington and West Drayton although at the time was used only for general purposes. The first railway to control trains by telegraph was the London & Blackwall in 1840, albeit with rope propulsion, not locomotives, and over a short self-contained line.

Telegraph lines were subsequently laid alongside railway lines for military and commercial uses. In 1847, a telegraph line was laid alongside the South Eastern Railway (SER) between Lewisham and London Bridge. It signalled Greenwich Mean Time from the Royal Observatory, eventually to the rest of the world. It also allowed Standard Railway Time to be established throughout Britain in 1852.

Block Working

To supersede time interval working, William Cooke introduced the idea of block working during the 1840s. This divided the track into blocks (sections) with signalmen communicating by telegraph to identify an approaching train and whether the line was clear to accept it.

One of the first to adopt the Block System was Charles Walker, Telegraph Superintendent of the SER. Starting in 1852 between London Bridge and Spa Road, it was extended to cover nearly all of the SER. The system used bell beats and pauses as coded messages for what was approaching and whether the line was clear. The receiving signalman had to repeat each message and both signalmen had to log it in their respective Train Register.

It was Walker who introduced the miniature signal arm which he combined with a bell in a single case, patented in 1865. The system worked well in suburbia where the stations were closely packed. For more widely spaced stations in the countryside, intermediate signal boxes were built to create block distances of up to 2 miles and so increase line capacity. Walker continued to design and develop various signalling instruments that were used in the days of mechanical signalling, one of the best known being his Train Describer.

Charles Vincent Walker (1812–1882)

Walker was an author of books and articles on electricity, magnetism, meteorology and the telegraph. He became Telegraph Engineer to the SER in 1845 where he invented the block system. His instruments were adopted throughout the world. Among his other inventions were telegraph wire insulation, improvement of batteries, the transmission of GMT, the rotary 12-position Train Describer and a submarine communications cable.

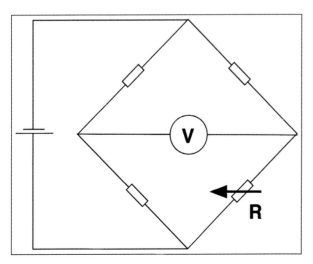
Wheatstone Bridge.

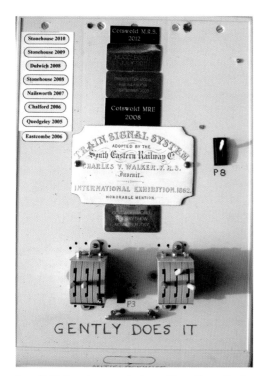

As a slight diversion, a control panel from the author's 'Brockley Acres' Model Railway. It features an enamelled plaque from one of Charles Walker's block devices. Model Railways are particularly prone to operator irregularities. We adhere to our own 'Very Permissive' block working and never log anything.

Multiple telegraph wires in Clapham cutting. They followed the main lines all the way to Southampton, Portsmouth and Exeter.

Permissive Block System

The block system spread to many railways. It worked well but was not foolproof. Indeed, some companies allowed Permissive Block Working whereby a second train could proceed with caution while the block was still occupied. On the London, Brighton & South Coast Railway (LB&SCR), the Permissive system was abandoned after a three-train crash in Clayton tunnel in 1861 due to misunderstandings between signalmen. Permissive block working, though, persisted on lines not used by passenger trains.

Absolute Block System

This strictly adhered to one train at a time on each block. Although 'absolute' in theory, it still relied on the proficiency of the signalman to apply it correctly. Irregular practices were possible, culminating in Britain's worst accident at Quintinshill in 1915, again involving three trains.

Sykes Lock and Block

To prevent irregular practices, William Sykes of the London, Chatham & Dover Railway (LC&DR) invented the Lock and Block system. His first step was to interlock the signals and points using a Saxby lever frame to prevent conflicting movements. His next step was to change the practice of signals being 'normally Off' to signals being 'normally at Danger'. His patented instrument was a wooden box connected physically to a signal lever. There were many versions, two of which are illustrated above.

The question now is – how many readers wish to understand the many variations and fine detail of how the systems worked? Like Company Directors, my guess is that it is sufficient for the average reader to appreciate just the broad principles of the Lock and Block. Technical details are well documented in References 1, 2 and 3.

William Robert Sykes (1840–1917)

At the age of 14, Sykes started work with the Electric and International Telegraph Company. In 1861 he moved to Shepherds, an electric clock and chronograph maker. He joined the LC&DR's Telegraph Department in 1863, rising to Superintendent. He is best remembered for his Lock and Block System but he also invented electro-mechanical signalling and slide switches. He experimented with track circuitry on the LC&DR and provided a system on the District Railway whereby signals turned automatically to red as trains passed them. In 1862 he founded W. R. Sykes Interlocking Signal Company with works at Clapham and Peckham. It went public in 1907.

Saxby & Farmer

John Saxby (1821–1913) worked on signalling for the LB&SCR. He was the first to patent an interlocking lever frame, the first example of which was at Victoria in 1860. One year later, he set up his own signalling company whose works were at Haywards Heath.

John Stinson Farmer (1827-1892) was Assistant Traffic Manager of the LB&SCR. In 1861 he joined John Saxby to found Saxby & Farmer. Their works at Kilburn eventually employed 3,000 workers. They also established a works in Brussels while James Saxby, his son, established a works at Criel, France. John Saxby left his own company in 1888 to manage the Criel works. In 1903 Saxby & Farmer merged with Evans O'Donnell and Co of Chippenham.

Users of Sykes Lock and Block

Mechanical locking mechanisms beneath lever frames, together with Lock and Block instruments, were costly to install. The cost was justified, however, by needing fewer signalmen and by making the railway safer – although the latter was necessarily difficult to quantify.

Sykes Lock and Block was installed on most of the LC&DR, SER and LB&SCR and on many other railways. The L&SWR was different, firstly for using a mix of Sykes and a rival system supplied by Preece, and secondly for using Lock and Block in a non-standard way. Ref. 1 includes a detailed description of how the L&SWR method worked. Charles Anderson (Ref. 4) sums it up as follows: 'All the L&SWR did was to adapt the time interval system to block conditions'. Anderson also observed a shortage

of Train Describers on the L&SWR. They had only two, resulting in complicated code ringing. (Train Describers were later commonplace on the Southern Railway.)

Limitations of Sykes Lock and Block

Until the advent of electronics, there was no safer system than Sykes Lock and Block. Indeed, it continued to be used into the BR era and beyond. Even so, it had its limitations. It could not prevent trains passing signals at Danger, as happened, for example, at St Johns in 1957 when a train passed three signals at Danger. Nor could it detect faulty equipment as happened, for example, at Clapham Junction in 1988 when a loose wire changed a colour light from red to green.

Two of the instruments supplied by William Sykes to the Somerset & Dorset Joint Railway (S&DJR). In the first picture, this Indicator Lock Instrument might typically have been used for a starting signal from a station. In the circular window, a metal tablet moves up and down to display 'Locked' in red or 'Free' in white. It remains Locked until an electrical signal that the train has left the block. This is sent from a treadle in the track just past the signal. The tablet is fixed to a lock blade which extends through the bottom of the instrument to the signal lever. A solenoid holds the blade up until the Free message is received, then it falls by gravity.

This Plunger Lock Instrument is from the Somerset & Dorset line and has two tablets, a plunger, a switch hook and a release key. When the Wellow box telegraphs 'Is Line Clear', this signalman acknowledges and presses the plunger. That unblocks the Wellow signal and this bottom tablet changes from Clear to Train On. When Wellow signals 'Train Entering Section', this signalman rotates the switch hook onto the plunger shaft and acknowledges. The procedure is repeated to the next box whose switch hook changes this upper tablet from Locked to Clear so that the signal can be pulled. When the train is beyond the treadle, the upper tablet reverts to Locked. The signal and switch hook can then be restored and the Wellow block becomes Clear. *Both photos: courtesy of West Country Rail Archives*

St Johns 'B' signal box was located in the vee of the junction. Ref. 5 includes a full description of the St Johns track arrangements in the early 1900s. *Crecy Transport Heritage Library*

But the Sykes instruments also had an Achilles heel: this was its Release Key. This could be used to release the lock blade to the 'Free' position in the event, for example, of the treadle failing to release, or of a shunting train not reaching the treadle. There were strict instructions before the release key could be used, one of these being if a train had been accepted and the signals cleared but then, for whatever reason, the train did not proceed. Under these circumstances it was perfectly legitimate to restore the system, although the signalman had to make the appropriate entry in the Train Register.

Irregular use of the Release Key resulted in a number of accidents. The SR's worst accident was at South Croydon in 1947 when an inexperienced signalman used the Release Key to admit a second train into a block, believing the apparatus to be faulty.

A common contributory cause at both St Johns and South Croydon was thick fog. Further contributory causes at St Johns were (a) the location of signals on the 'wrong' side of the track for SR steam engines and (b) the lack of provision on the 12-position Train Describers for the new Hastings DEMUs. This resulted in the next signalman stopping the mystery train until recognised and another train being stopped behind it – the one that was rammed. Setting signalling budgets is a delicate balancing act that can result in disaster if set too low. There is always a ceiling on expenditure and no transport system is ever absolutely safe. It is a ratcheting process towards 'safer'.

SE&CR Developments

The SE&CR installed many new Sykes systems together with electro-mechanical signalling; an example is shown in the accompanying illustration of St Johns 'B' signal box. On the top level are the block bells and a row of what is mainly miniature repeater signals. On the next row down, the white rectangular panels appear to indicate whether points have been set correctly for particular signal levers to be pulled. Below the maker's nameplate are three-position indicators for Train On/ Normal/ Clear into the next blocks, then another row of white rectangles.

Top right are two Walker's Receiving Train Describers. Between the two Walker's Sending Train Describers (with handles) are five windows with Locked/Free tablets. Slides for the electro-mechanical signals are next, then the plungers and bell pushes and finally the point levers. The operation of the train describers is best quoted from the LBSCR rule book which states: 'The lever at the description required must be pulled forward and the lever where the pointer is then resting is put

Still in the style of Sykes, the standard SR Lock & Block instrument was in common use for some 80 years. The plunger has been replaced by a rotary handle, which moves between three positions to operate electric circuits. Left to right: 'Train on Line (red segment), 'Normal' (white segment) and 'Line Clear' (green segment). Instead of a switch hook, there is a sliding brass plate. A Sidmouth Junc. nameplate has been added to this anonymous example. *Photo: courtesy of West Country Rail Archives*

back; the pointer will then move to the description required and remain there until the next train is described.' Note that the required description will be repeated at the box in advance so the signalman is made aware of the destination of the next train, the type of train being conveyed by the bell code used. In this case it would also be more accurate to describe the instruments as 'route describers' as the indications refer to the route/destination of the train rather than the type of service. In other locations, and indeed on other railways, 'Train describers' were exactly that – a description of the type of train that was being sent.

Southern Railway Developments

The SR continued to install new Sykes instruments together with electro-mechanical signalling. Sykes slides were later superseded in favour of Westinghouse miniature levers and interlock relays were introduced instead of heavy frames. The first four-aspect colour lights in the world were installed in 1926 between Holborn Viaduct and Elephant & Castle, also at Cannon Street and Charing Cross. The SE&CR had pioneered three-position semaphores at Victoria and these too were superseded by colour lights.

Westinghouse

In 1920, Saxby & Farmer and Sykes merged with the Westinghouse Air Brake Company and other signal companies including McKenzie & Holland and Dutton. The new name was the Westinghouse Brake and Saxby Signal Company. This was shortened in 1935 to Westinghouse Brake & Signal. After further mergers and take-overs, the company today is Siemens Rail Automation Limited.

These two views show Westinghouse equipment installed at Balham in 1952. Instead of Walker rotaries, the train describers are vertical with light bulbs and instead of Sykes slide switches, points and signals are operated by miniature levers. Other changes are that instead of Sykes indicators, there are roundels above the levers which repeat the indication of the colour light signals (three or four multiple aspect indications) or show point status. Also, instead of a mechanical interlocking frame, there is a relay room. There are still bell pushes for emergency use but under normal circumstances the signalman now relied on track circuitry for information of 'Line Clear'. *John Hinson, made available through his Studio433 website*

Weighing nearly 23 tons, the heaviest mechanical interlocking frame ever built was at London Bridge in 1928. The first box with relays was North Kent East in 1929, itself a pioneer venture which would eventually be taken forward by BR with the development of solid state interlocking instead of using relays

References

1. Anderson, Charles, *From LBSC to BR – Part 2 London (West)*, The Southern Way Issue 33.

2. Postlethwaite, Alan, *St Johns, Lewisham – History, Mystery and Connections*, The Southern Way Issue 8.

3. Pryer, G., *A Pictorial Record of Southern Signals*, Oxford Publishing Company, 1977.

4. thesignalbox website.

5. Vanns, Michael A., *An Illustrated History of Signalling*, Ian Allan Publishing, 1997.

6. Westinghouse Brake & Signal Company Ltd Miniature Power Lever Frames website.

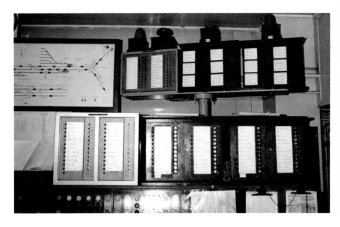

The Horton Light Railway
A Personal View
John Burgess

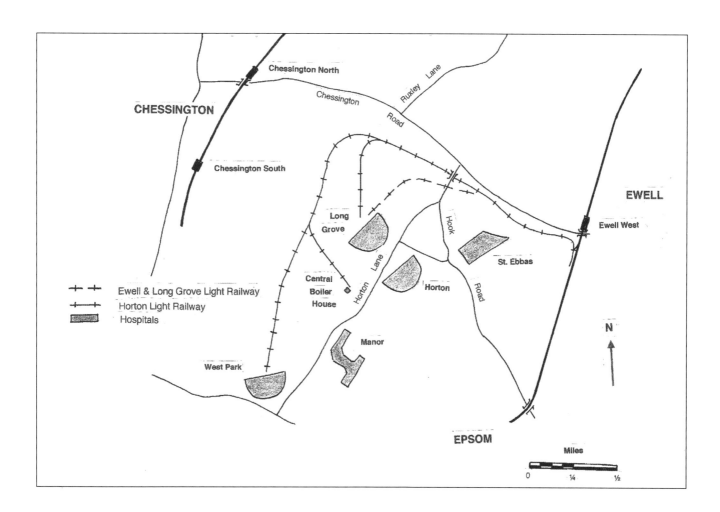

On the edge of West Ewell is what is now Horton Country Park, originally a private estate but which was purchased by the London County Council in 1896 with the intention of building six hospitals to house those who were considered to suffer from mental disorders. In the event only five hospitals were built but even so it is known several thousand persons were cared for, excluding nursing, auxiliary, domestic and maintenance staff. It was in effect a small and in some respects a self-contained town.

The first hospital was completed in 1899 and known as 'Manor' (all the hospitals were given names), but this was quickly found to be insufficient and a new contract was let to Messrs Charles Wall Ltd for the foundations of the next hospitals. With the work site some two miles away from the nearest station at Ewell West, materials and supplies were necessarily hauled by traction engine along inadequate roads

and it was not until November 1904, five years after the commencement, that the foundations alone were complete.

A new contract was let on 15 December 1904, Messrs Forster and Dicksee given until June 1907 to complete the actual superstructures. This firm was aware of the transport problems faced by their predecessors and so applied to the Board of Trade for permission to build a standard gauge line*, the Ewell & Long Grove Light Railway, from Ewell West to the Hospital site. Discussions involving several parties, likely over the crossing of a bridle path and also Hook Lane, took two months, but permission was granted and the new line was first used as early as 20 April 1905 when locomotive *Hollymoor* arrived at the work site with a train of bricks and cement from an interchange siding immediate south of the London & South Western's (LSWR) Ewell West station. For the 900 workmen arriving by trains at Ewell West from Waterloo, they mostly still had to walk the two and a half miles from the station as the railway was not officially approved to carry passengers. Meanwhile at the site, various sidings took the railway as close as possible to the various buildings. The structures were complete in April 1907, two months ahead of schedule.

Initially, two engines were used, *Hollymoor*, known locally as 'Puffing Billy', was a Manning Wardell 'K' class 0-6-0ST built in 1901 and used on the line until sold in early 1907. This engine was joined in 1904 by a Barclay 0-4-0ST (Andrew Barclay No 994) named *Crossness*; the livery of this machine was dark green.

With two engines, a rudimentary form of train control was required and this came in the form of a copper-plated train staff. A small loco shed was also provided (from what date is not known but likely early on) near what was known as 'Sherwood'. A man referred to as 'Oliver' and nicknamed 'red flag' was also employed at the road crossing at Hook Lane to warn other traffic of movement over what was locally known as the 'Forster & Dicksee's Railway'.

When complete, the 'Epsom Cluster' (as the hospitals were collectively referred to) housed over 7,000 residents. It was a massive investment in (social) care on a scale which, at the time, exceeded anything else comparable in Britain, possibly in the world, although the disruption caused during construction to the edge of Epsom must have been severe.

Not all the original lines built to carry construction material survived; one of these, the short lived Ewell & Long Grove Light Railway (E&LGLR)*, was provided just to support the building of Long Grove Hospital. Unfortunately, construction was not without incident, with a fatal accident reported to a resident of one of the hospitals, Mary Tobin, who was hit by a train crossing the Horton Road. This accident would have ramifications in later years.

The original E&LGLR closed after the building work had been completed and finding any trace of it on the ground is now virtually impossible although the odd earthwork may still be found near to Great Wood in the present day Country Park, a quite remarkable survivor for an obscure light railway which ran for just a few years and closed over 100 years ago.

The last of the hospital buildings was at West Park, but prior to construction, the London County Council had decided to update the existing route, which included an underbridge at Hook Road and the fencing off of the complete line. A footbridge was also erected over the Epsom to Ewell bridle path. The plan was also to extend the railway over what is Horton lane, so as to serve the Horton and Manor hospital sites but to do this the Board of Trade insisted a tunnel be constructed under Horton Lane rather than the proposed level crossing. The complications and cost associated with this meant the extension was never completed.

The Horton Light Railway* (HLR) was authorised in 1909, and opened in 1913. It ran from some extended exchange sidings near to West Ewell station (the site of which later became Surrey County Council's Highway House and adjoining highway depot, now both in turn replaced by new housing) parallel to Chessington Road until it reached Horton Lane. Here was the under bridge referred to, the remains of which still stand, although the road has been diverted and no longer runs over the bridge. This redundant bridge is the most substantial structure remaining of the former railway, and is a legacy of the Mary Tobin accident, as were a number of footbridges carrying public rights of way over the line.

During World War 1 the hospital complex came under the control of a War Committee and in March and April 1915 the residents were evacuated from the Horton site (we are not told where to) and the place made ready to receive wounded

Hollymoor, the original locomotive acquired for the short-lived Ewell & Long Grove Light Railway, propelling a train of wagons over the Hook Road level crossing heading towards the Long Grove building site. The green colour is conjectural – the few photographs suggest that it was painted a dark colour with just a hint of lining visible which I have chosen not to show. The crossing became the scene of the fatal accident involving Mary Tobin and the subsequent inquest gave some information about working practices, which are evident in the sketch. Gates were provided but hinged away from the road and apparently left open while trains were running. Warning signs reading 'Beware of the Trains' were erected. When propelling, the guard rode on one of the wagons but on the day of the accident he took up a position on the fifth wagon because the first four were sheeted over. In my view, he is on the sixth wagon from the locomotive. We may conclude then that brake vans were not used and so the presence of a 'Guard' was merely arbitrary.

A second view of the same crossing was later produced when it was pointed out that I had painted the locomotive the wrong way round! This sketch was painted in acrylic, and the viewpoint is from the opposite side of the crossing. Here the lookout is on the fifth wagon from the locomotive.

A view of *Crossness* used on the Horton Light Railway from 1913. It was built in 1904 and first used by the LCC at Crossness sewage works and came from the works of Andrew Barclay in Kilmarnock. It was replaced by *Hendon* in 1935, by which time it was worn out. According to the Industrial Record Society, it was painted dark green, perhaps darker than I have depicted it. The locomotive is standing on the siding leading to the boiler house at West Park Hospital, whose distinctive tall tower looms over the hospital. Photographs of the hospital were hard to find, so the picture is worked up from details found on old Ordnance Survey plans in conjunction with a few pictures found on the internet showing the hospital just before demolition. Beyond the hospital are the woods of Epsom Common, rising away to the south. The distinctive tower remains and is being converted into flats.

soldiers. Again, the idea of extending to Horton hospital was raised for the obvious purpose of running ambulance trains as close as possible. This time it was considered the gradients and curvature would be a difficulty and instead the wounded were conveyed in LSWR road vehicles from an offloading point at Epsom station.

Post World War 1 a new hospital at West Park was proposed whilst, in addition, a new power plant to provide electricity to the site was scheduled for a location known as Sherwood. The railway was extended to reach both of these points and at the latter was also the engine shed. This new route had a ruling gradient of 1 in 40 against loaded trains. Of note is that the LCC had at least two private owner wagons used for the disposal of ash. We are not told but presumably operation was still by train-staff.

Crossness was by now getting on in years and a replacement Manning Wardle 0-6-0ST, works number 2046, *Hendon* was obtained from previous work on LCC housing estates at Burnt Oak and St Helier. *Crossness* was then cut up, although pieces lay beside the locomotive shed for some time.

Quoting now from C. G. Down, 'Many and varied were the incidents affecting the line during the Second World War. At one time, three steam locomotives were noted in the sidings at Ewell West, two in black livery, the other green. These were probably resting there *en route* for some other destination, but it should be noted that once or twice locomotives were borrowed from the L.S.W.R. (and later the S.R.) when the L.C.C. engine was under repair; a member of the "P" class, an 0-6-0T, a type having a short wheel base, was known to have been used. Three bomb incidents are of note. Once, the engine crew arrived to find that the locomotive shed had collapsed and was solely supported by its inmate; bomb splinters on one occasion removed several portions of *Hendon*, while an unexploded bomb which had lain unnoticed by the lineside exploded a short while after the passage of a train, removing a large portion of the track and earthworks.'

Post-World War 2 *Hendon* needed a new firebox – presumably the hospital, being basically self-contained, retained maintenance staff for the locomotives as well – but instead of a repair, another new engine was obtained. This was *Sherwood* and came from Robert Stephenson & Hawthorns Ltd in November 1944.

Sherwood was an 0-4-0ST. Again quoting C. G. Down, '*Hendon*, which had in the meanwhile been sold to A. R. Adams of Newport, was found to be, in retrospect, the best locomotive of the line's stud. *Sherwood* was totally unsuited to the long hard run. She was a poor steamer and after only a few months' running her slide bars had become badly worn. Nevertheless, her life was not without incident for the local youth was active and she was derailed several times by stones in the points or by sleepers placed across the rails. Once, during a fog, *Sherwood* ran full-tilt into an ash-truck which someone had pushed under the Hook Road bridge; fortunately she was not derailed.'

Maintenance of the permanent way seems also to have been limited at this time and there was a need to have the track renewed. An attempt was made to secure this in the form of an exercise given to the Royal Engineers but this fell through and the decision was instead made to close the railway in January 1950. The remains, including *Sherwood*, were salvaged by G. Cohen and Sons for, according to the *Epsom Herald*, £8,371, *Sherwood* being sold to a firm in Coleford but later reported at Widnes.

The Route Described

The railway started a few yards from Ewell West station and commenced its independent passage a few yards behind the Highways depot. Passing through a gate denoting the end of railway property, it then crossed the River Hogsmill and began to climb past a recreation ground and the Epsom to Ewell bridle path. There was then a level stretch between the boundary fence of St Ebbas hospital and the rear garden of houses in Chessington Road before the drop to the bridge under the Hook Road. The distance so far was one mile. There was now a low embankment before a curve west to pass through the wooded but marshy Butcher's Grove. At the one-and-a-half-mile point came the junction taking the railway either to Sherwood/West Park or Longrove. The Longrove line continued for three-quarters of a mile to the hospital of that name. The route to West Park was of a switchback nature until it reached a passing loop, which was also the point of divergence to Sherwood, itself the continuation of what was the most level part of the line. That to West Park was on a low embankment lined with trees and hedges for about three-quarters of a mile before passing under a footbridge and entering the gates of West Park hospital

Today and to the north of Horton Lane, the route has been redeveloped as a car park to Horton Golf Club, but beyond this the way is clear and much has been turned into public paths by the Council, providing easy walks through the Country Park. The original boiler house chimney and water tower still stand at West Park Hospital, as a prominent landmark and indicator of the furthest-most reach of the line. The Longrove hospital branch is interrupted by the Golf Course and has been partially diverted. Evidence of the junctions is still apparent where loops were installed to enable wagons to be run round and then be propelled down the branches for unloading. This is supported by noting where the formation widens out slightly.

Being a former railway line, the paths are relatively flat and well engineered. In places, the route is raised above the surrounding land on low embankments, and walking is easy going.

This is *Hendon* bringing a train of empty wagons back from the Central Boiler House under one of several footbridges along the line, all trace of which has now gone. These footbridges were flanked with high fences probably to protect the public from the sight of the strange antics of the hospital residents and to give the residents some degree of privacy. The red livery of the locomotive is an intelligent guess at the appearance of this engine but I may have got it wrong and if anybody has other views I would be happy to hear from them. In the background are two superb elm trees, also now a thing of the past but once common here. The view is looking towards West Park Farm, and the track bed as far as the footbridge is now a public path, joining the footpath running across the picture. To this day there is a substantial white post hidden away in the verge where the paths meet which has all the appearance of an old gate post protecting a level crossing, perhaps used by farm vehicles in days gone by? Track work was flat-bottom rail laid either on wooden or concrete sleepers.

Later Days

The railway ran a daily goods service, mainly taking in coal. It survived World War 2, but, as stated, by the end of the war was in a very poor condition. Ownership also passed from London County Council to the newly created National Health Service and there appears to have been little appetite to keep it open. The railway closed in 1950, and was dismantled shortly after. Although gone, it is not forgotten and Epsom and Ewell Borough Council have produced a very informative leaflet packed with photographs taken over 60 years ago illustrating the railway, mainly from the collections of R. Roberts and N. Davenport. From time to time, the Country Park staff also arrange organised walks and illustrated talks.

Care-wise too, times change and by the 1970s the writing was on the wall for these large and rather forbidding institutions. The farms closed first, with Epsom and Ewell Borough Council acquiring much of the land to the west of Horton Lane, which formed the basis for the present day Country Park. There were two farms here (Long Grove and West Park), together with various parcels of woodland.

Today, Horton Country Park is busy with visitors. The main paths are well used by pedestrians and dog walkers, joggers, cyclists and horse riders. Despite this activity on the main routes, it is possible to get away from the crowds into the remoter parts of the Country Park, perhaps sit on a bench and imagine the sound of the distant whistle of the daily freight as it brings in a new consignment of coal for the hospitals.

*The reference to a 'light' railway is a bit misleading as none of the lines built complied exactly with the 1896 Light Railways Act, which was intended to refer to passenger-carrying lines. In this case the word 'light' should be taken to have a literal railway meaning, as a railway with limited engineering and intended to serve a freight rather than a passenger purpose. Certainly there was never any passenger accommodation used to transport patients or visitors to or around the site, compared with, for example, the early days of the hospital railway at Hellingly.

References

Down, C. G., 'Horton Estate Light Railway' – *The Industrial Railway Record* No 13, 1967. Article available on the Internet at www.irsociety.co.uk Also letter in issue No 18 with additional photographs, available on the same website.

Essen, R. I., *Epsom's Hospital Railway*, self published, 1991.

'Horton Country Park Local Nature Reserve – Days of Steam', Epsom and Ewell Borough Council – Leaflet.

Jackson, A. Alan, *Railways of Surrey*, Atlantic Transport Publishers, 1999.

Jux, Frank and Hateley, Roger, *Industrial Railways and Locomotives of Sussex and Surrey*, published by the Industrial Railway Society, 2015.

Mitchell, Vic and Smith, Keith, *London Suburban Railways – Wimbledon to Epsom*, Middleton Press, 1995.

Winfield, Nick, 'Railways serving the Epsom Cluster', www.epsomandewellhistoryexplorer.org.uk

Sherwood, for which the nameplates were cast but never carried, shunting a few wagons at the Ewell West exchange sidings. In the up reception siding is a Southern Railway 'W' class 2-6-4T, and a conversation is going on across the fence. I have shown *Sherwood* in a two-tone green livery with black/white lining, which is conjectural but fits with various photographs of this engine. For a time, this locomotive appears with a hole in the rear cab sheeting to accommodate the brake handle. Later, this was covered with a neat box. This engine is the only object with a touch of colour on a bleak, misty winter day between 1948 and closure. The permanent way was badly neglected in the last few years, and here the HLR tracks, infested with weeds, contrast with the neat appearance of the main line side of the fence.

Maunsell's Pièce de Résistance
The 'Schools' Class
with Particular Reference to the Personalities
and Politics Behind the Design

Jeremy Clarke

Some time ago a friend commented that he thought it was Oliver Bulleid who had said something to the effect that designing a successful steam engine was largely the art of making compromises. I disagreed, not about the compromises but that Bulleid, that most uncompromising of locomotive engineers, would have said any such thing. (The popular and well-respected Inspector Danny Knight, who accompanied Southern crews during the 1948 Exchange Trials, is known to have once said that Bulleid was a brilliant engineer although not a practical one.) But could Richard Maunsell have expressed a similar opinion? Given the conditions under which he worked, when much of the Southern's motive power expenditure went on electrification, it is possible.

Before looking at the compromises he did have to make in the most successful of his engines, a note about the man himself. My late friend A. B. MacLeod told me that Richard Edward Lloyd Maunsell (RELM) would get very cross indeed if someone pronounced his name as 'Mawnsell'. It was 'Mansell' and on that there was never any compromise, the 'u' being superfluous in the pronunciation. His Norman antecedents were assigned 'Mauncel' or 'Maunsel' Manor in Somerset following the Conquest and in the 13th century the member of the family then holding it assumed the name as his own. The Gloucestershire village of Frampton Mansell was among those held by the manor as the suffix implies but appears never to have had the intrusive 'u' in its title. It lies some six miles ESE of Stroud and gives its name to Frampton level crossing, ½-mile west of Sapperton Tunnel on the Golden Valley line between Swindon and Gloucester.

Meanwhile, some of the Maunsell family had moved to Ireland where more property was granted them. Richard Edward Lloyd Maunsell came from that branch, being born at Raheny, Co Dublin, on 26 May 1868.

Maunsell was widely experienced by the time the newly created Southern Railway (SR) confirmed his appointment as Chief Mechanical Engineer having started his engineering career on the Great Southern & Western Railway, before

The doyen of the type, No 900 Eton as outshopped in March 1930. Likely every member of the class was similarly photographed in what was then standard 'works grey' with the background removed. After an active life of 30 years it was stored at Brighton from October 1960 until March 1962 before being withdrawn and dismantled at Ashford the following month. *SR Official*

Seen from the opposite side, this is No 907 Dulwich (built July 1930) at New Cross shed, 21 March 1931. Active until September 1961, the engine had even received a new firebox in December 1959 but was deemed surplus to requirements and was also reduced to scrap at Ashford. *E. R. Wethersett*

continuing on the Lancashire & Yorkshire and subsequently on the East India Railway. At the time 1923, he was 54 years of age and had been in charge at the South Eastern & Chatham Railway's (SECR) Ashford works since 1 December 1913. By comparison, Robert Urie of the London & South Western Railway (LSWR) was in his 69th year while Lawson Billinton of the London, Brighton & South Coast Railway (LBSCR) was just approaching 40. In view of his advancing years and thus the limited time he could serve, Urie had sensibly declined the post, offered to him first on the basis presumably of his seniority. (A similar scenario applied on the newly formed London & North Eastern Railway where J. G. Robinson of the Great Central also declined the top post, so leaving the way clear for Nigel Gresley to take charge.) Billinton had the disadvantage of being 'Brighton' through-and-through with little experience beyond it though he had proved himself a capable engineer and an excellent man-manager following a difficult time in the Brighton's history. To his further disadvantage he had been away on military service for much of the time leading up to Grouping though within that period he spent time on railway missions in Russia and Eastern Europe as Lt-Col Lawson Billinton RE. His military service had concluded on 2 August 1918 but the Army recalled him three months later for a further mission to Romanian State Railways, hence he did not resume his LBSCR career until August 1919. (He was later made CBE for this post-war work.) There was

thus little doubt in the minds of the Southern Board which of those two should be chosen.

Maunsell, first and foremost, was an excellent administrator with a firmly established and wide engineering background, theoretical as well as practical, including his experience elsewhere. He had shown himself capable of producing some excellent locomotives on a tight budget and had successfully resolved the chaotic situation at Ashford Works following his appointment there. His predecessor at Ashford, Harry Wainwright, it seems, had been unable to manage successfully the move from Carriage & Wagon Superintendent of the South Eastern Railway (SER) to the much larger responsibility of Locomotive, Carriage & Wagon Superintendent of the combined companies following the transfer of personnel and equipment from the Chatham's factory at Longhedge. Being essentially a carriage and wagon man, although he had an interest in boilers, Wainwright left much of the locomotive design work to his Chief Draughtsman, the vastly experienced Robert Surtees. Indeed, there is evidence of Surtees' position in the form of a photographic postcard of a 'D' class 4-4-0 signed by the man himself and dated 1899, the class not actually coming into service until 1901. His failures saw Wainwright effectively fired even if his departure in 1913 was euphemistically described as retirement on health grounds. (Perhaps that was actually true for he died at the age of 60 in September 1925.)

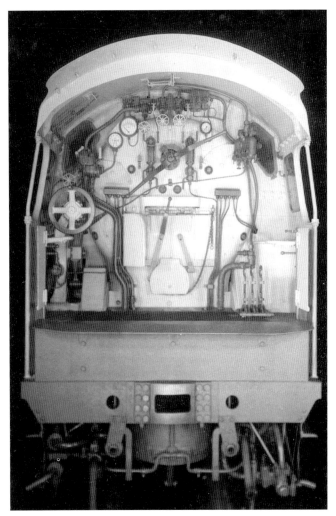

The people Maunsell recruited to join his design team both before and after Grouping illustrates his keen interest in developments beyond his immediate responsibility. In addition, his ability to delegate and closely supervise but not interfere had already been proven. Compare the activities of Wainwright's Chief Clerk Hugh McColl, who took 'supervision' rather too literally, as O. S. Nock puts it, 'wielding almost absolute power and ruling the Running Department' – part of the Locomotive Superintendent's responsibilities at that time – 'with a rod of iron'. Wainwright, more concerned with trying to master his much enlarged department and get it properly funded, had allowed McColl too much freedom: Maunsell did not. It is written McColl mellowed under Maunsell. It seems more likely he had much less influence having been stripped of his power to bully.

On his appointment to the SR's top mechanical post, Maunsell had responsibility for 2,285 engines in no fewer than 115 different classes. 4-4-0s and 0-6-0s, both tank and tender, predominated and other than Billinton's 'Baltic'

Original cab view when new (the specific engine is not identified). Left-hand drive, and wheel reverser. Various modifications and additions were made to some, but certainly not all, engines over the years. These included AWS, speedometer and water treatment. For details of specific engines the reader is referred to the excellent *Book of the Schools* by Richard Derry (Irwell Press) and D. L. Bradley's, *Locomotives of the Southern Railway by the RCTS*.

Below: No E908 *Westminster* (renumbered as plain '908' in September 1931) seen soon after building in July 1930. Possibly the man with the trilby is an inspector ready to observe the performance at first hand. The addition of smoke deflectors was subsequently deemed necessary in response to complaints, their fixture, as will be seen in subsequent views, a necessity even if subjective so far as aesthetics were concerned. *LPC*

tanks only the South Western provided relatively large engines, mostly emanating from Urie's time in charge. But there were also ancients as, for example, Stroudley 'Terriers' from 1872, the three Beattie 2-4-0 well tanks of 1874 lodged in their faraway North Cornish stronghold and much rebuilt in the interim, and some worn out oddities on the Isle of Wight. But among the best engines were the general-purpose 'N' class Moguls from Maunsell's own Ashford stable with its Swindonian influence, and the classic 'rebuilds' of Classes E1 and D1. Just how different things might have been had he been given the same freedom to improve the locomotive stock as Stanier received 10 years later on the LMS under Josiah Stamp's chairmanship is impossible to know. But judging by the success Maunsell attained with the final development of the classic British 4-4-0, the 'V' or 'School's class, it would no doubt have been well worth recording.

Maunsell's earlier 4-4-0, the 'L1', was symptomatic of his problems from the start. This class was essentially Wainwright's 'L' of 1913 with the minimum of modifications, the main ones being smaller cylinders, a higher boiler pressure and a Maunsell superheater as well as some cosmetic changes. Unlike the 'D' and 'E' rebuilds there was not time before they were required for traffic to fully redesign the valve gear, though that did not stop them being both fast and powerful engines. But how much better might they have been with that modification? Moreover, the class was limited to 15 examples, supplied by North British between March and May 1926. Three or four times that number would have reduced the unit cost and permitted withdrawal of many inefficient late 19th century pre-Grouping engines, some of which were still knocking about

– in both senses of the phrase! – into BR days. Perhaps as an indication of that restricted order, Ashford rebuilt nine more 'D's to 'D1' between November 1926 and July 1927.

Hamilton Ellis commented that Drummond built engines as solid as a battleship: his erstwhile Chief Draughtsman, Robert Urie, followed that example. The remodelled 'N15', the 'King Arthur' – what an inspired piece of publicity on John Elliott's part! – and 'S15' were both outstanding classes in their fields. No 777, *Sir Lamiel*, proved very popular with 'foreign' crews who handled her on tour in preservation, appreciating the engine's simplicity, steaming ability and sure-footedness. Derek Cross once described the class as the prototype for the LMS 'Black Five', whilst Stephen Townroe during his time in charge at Eastleigh was known to prefer the predictive performance of the 'King Arthur' type to the totally unpredictable behaviour of the original Bulleid designs.

Slight exaggeration so far as the prototype for the 'Black 5' perhaps but surely with an element of truth. Once, in preservation, *Sir Lamiel* stalled in horrible rail conditions on the 1 in 80 of Honiton Bank while working a special to Exeter. But in a real show of strength successfully restarted the 400-ton train after some of the support crew had cleaned and sanded the rails for some distance ahead. (It is believed they were then left behind as, once away, the train would not stop for them. In any event it was already seriously delaying a regular up service waiting and champing at the bit in the loop at Honiton station!) The various preservation societies that managed to get their hands on an 'S15' and return it to running order are similarly no doubt grateful for both the power and reliability of the class.

No 902 *Wellington* on the 8.25am from Charing Cross recorded at Waterloo High Level (later Waterloo East). The top half of the smoke deflectors is painted green, another point where opinions vary as to appearance. *J. G. Reynolds*

Returning to 1923, Maunsell's first task was to assess the locomotive stock, this despite the fact that the full senior management team of the new company had yet to be established. Indeed, for the first few months all three General Managers from the main constituents of the Southern were jointly responsible. However, William Forbes, formerly of the Brighton, retired at the end of June 1923 and Percy Tempest of the SECR followed him at the year's end, leaving Herbert Walker of the LSWR to hold office until 1937.

It is probable Walker had already advised Maunsell – if he did not already know it – a large proportion of the capital budget would be allocated to electrification. Maunsell had, too, to meld the three main workshops, Ashford, Brighton and Eastleigh as well as the Brighton carriage works at Lancing, and their staffs into a cohesive and sustainable unit. Thomas Finlayson, the chief draughtsman at Eastleigh, proved the most difficult to handle. He would simply ignore instructions or changes to drawings required by Maunsell's senior staff, Holcroft or Clayton for example, that is if they didn't conform to his own design principles – prejudices? But he could not ignore instructions issued by Maunsell himself: to save time and argument that's how things were then often done. Nevertheless, Holcroft still contends Finlayson exerted influence simply by bringing ideas of his own to bear and arguing to Clayton particularly that they were preferable to whatever had been put forward. Finlayson epitomised 'the canny Scot', for following his first period at Ashford, Clayton had spent his most influential years at Derby with its 'small engine' policy dictated by the 'Running' side of the organisation. To support his view Holcroft believes Finlayson made the 'Lord Nelsons' far more of an Eastleigh product than

Maunsell might have liked by playing on Clayton's lack of experience in the designing and building of big engines. Finlayson had soon discovered that, once persuaded, Clayton's advice to Maunsell would almost always be accepted. But Holcroft concedes the 'Nelson' was among the most reliable and economical of classes. (An ex-fireman friend would certainly endorse the latter point, stating that he'd fire to a 'Nelson' only about 70% of the coal required for the same job by a 'West Country'.)

One early problem Maunsell tackled also concerned Eastleigh. He found that, contrary to safe practice, the larger engines were often weighed without the required full boiler of water and an average load of coal on the grate. The reason for the deviation was, apparently, to ensure the Civil Engineer's prescribed maximum axleload of 20 tons would not be exceeded. No doubt somebody in the Works felt the full fury of an unleashed Irish temper for, to Maunsell, this was undoubtedly a deception at the highest level and a potentially dangerous one at that. He ordered all engines be reweighed in the proper condition as a matter of urgency with the chief draughtsman present to see that they were, and all revised data so obtained to be immediately sent to him at Waterloo.

When it came to the 'V', an engine built in response to the general specification of '400 tons at an average of 55mph', much design work was again deputed to Eastleigh. By contrast to the 'Nelson' can one perhaps discern Clayton's influence here with the 'small engine' 4-4-0 chassis configuration being favoured, albeit a hefty 4-4-0? This wheel arrangement had successfully figured in British locomotive practice for years and many commentators regarded it as the ideal from the handling and maintenance aspects.

No 932 *Blundell's* **on a down Waterloo to Basingstoke stopper recorded west of Woking. Note the high-sided tender. This was another engine that spent some time in store before official withdrawal. It was almost as if there was a reluctance to condemn what was a class of excellent engines.** *M. W. Earley*

The first outline for the 'V', a designation subsequently almost lost under the generally referred-to title of 'Schools', included a Belpaire firebox and a boiler on the same lines as the 'Nelson', though naturally modified in view of the shorter frame. It is recorded Finlayson had an intense dislike of Belpaires and, characteristically, tried to persuade Clayton to discard it. Having lost the fight with the 'Nelson' he perhaps thought working in a Belpaire all over again on this new engine was a bit too much! No doubt when a later modified specification was received, that the engine should conform to the 'Hastings Line' loading gauge, Finlayson may well have felt the point had been conceded. The fact was, of course, the modification had been requested by the operators and that's what put a Belpaire firebox out of the equation.

The width restriction south of Tunbridge Wells arose from a piece of spivery by the contractor. In 1862 it was found Mountfield tunnel was in danger of collapse, inspection showing only one ring of brickwork had been put in rather than the four specified, a shocking example of lax supervision on the part of the Resident Engineer. In October that year authorisation was given for relining this and other tunnels found in similar condition but rather than cut out and enlarge to the original specification much of the new lining was put on top of the existing brickwork. Although this had little immediate effect on the rolling stock being used at the time, it later required batches of 'slim line' coaches and motive power to be provided explicitly for the line. The handy Moguls of 'N' and 'U' classes for example – 8ft 8in over cylinders – were banned but their 'N1' and 'U1' brethren, with their width-restricted three-cylinder layout at 8ft 6½in were not. (What a difference just 1½in could make.) Even some goods vehicles were prohibited, as were carriages with duckets to the guards' compartments.

It is recorded only just a slight inaccuracy in spacing during track renewal in Mountfield tunnel once saw swathes of door handles ripped off two trains passing one another there. Use of standard-size stock on electrification of the line in 1986 required track through the four tunnels, Somerhill, Strawberry Hill, Wadhurst and Mountfield, to be singled.

Apart from the problems of clearance the Hastings line abounds in curves as well as sharp gradients. Aside from the long climbs through the North Downs to Knockholt on the 1868 main line, from St Johns going down and from Tonbridge coming up, there are other summits at Wadhurst, Mountfield Tunnel and Battle. Besides those, the 6½-mile climb to Somerhill Tunnel off the platform end at Tonbridge, including the wicked 1 in 53/47 at the start, is taxing in the extreme, especially as, even for non-stop trains, the sharp curve through and after the East junction at Tonbridge precludes a run being taken at it. (If you get the opportunity to listen to Peter Handford's recording made from the train of a 'School' over this steepest stretch, go for it: the 'music' is glorious!)

Like the specification in general, the shorter 4-4-0 chassis remained though I wonder if Maunsell now contemplated a six-coupled one for this difficult road in view of the potentially greater adhesion it offered. But the short chassis was cheaper to build and maintain, reduced the overhang on curves and had less internal resistance, that is, it lost less of its power moving itself than a six-coupled engine would. Moreover, St Leonards shed, where allocation and servicing would inevitably be made, only had a turntable of 50 feet in diameter, hand operated at that. The answer then was to ally this chassis with as much of the bigger 'Nelson's' mechanical parts as possible but mount on it a 'King Arthur'-type boiler and its accompanying round-top firebox. Finlayson must have been delighted!

Early BR days, and No 30938 *St Olave's* passes Teynham with the down 'Kentish Belle'. This engine was allocated to Bricklayers Arms from New, remaining there until June 1958. After that it was moved on a yearly basis to Stewarts Lane, Ashford and Dover before reaching Nine Elms in May 1961. Here it had just two months of work – we assume it was used – before being withdrawn in July 1961.
P. Ransome-Wallis

The outcome was a locomotive that truly epitomised the old adage that 'if it looks right, it is right'. There is little doubt that from an artistic point of view the 'Schools' were the most aesthetically pleasing and balanced of engines. (May I amend that a little and exclude those later fitted with the Lemaître exhaust and its ugly chimney and, perhaps also, the later addition of smoke deflectors? *(Be wary Jeremy – I and suspect others would contend that the addition of smoke-deflectors actually enhanced their looks. But we will agree on that chimney! – Ed.)* That look was matched by the new tender designed for it, of the same basic dimensions as that attached to the later 'King Arthurs' and the 'L1' and 'Q' classes but with slightly higher sides to accommodate a tank capacity increased from 3,500 to 4,000 gallons. The bunker, as before, could hold five tons of coal.

From the 'Nelson' came the 22-spoke, 6ft 7in driving wheels on a 10ft wheelbase though the diameter had emanated as a Nine Elms/Eastleigh 'standard' many years before. Balance weights covered five spokes in the trailing pair and six on the leading ones where, of course, the big ends and cranks for the valve gear were mounted. The bogie had 3ft 1in wheels, again an Eastleigh standard, with 10 spokes. The three Nelson cylinders were 16½in diameter by 26in stroke fed by 8in-diameter piston valves. Unlike the 'Nelson', in which the inside cylinders were pitched forward to drive the leading axle, those of the 'School' were in line. Weights were significant, 21 tons on each driving axle and no less than 25 tons (2cwt+) on the massive bogie of 7ft 6in wheelbase. Neither the 'N15' nor the 'LN' registered an axleload of 21 tons and it may have been only

because the 'V' had the three-cylinder layout which, being almost self-balancing, reduced the hammer blow that that weight was permitted. Individual Walschaerts gear was provided for all three valves though it has been rumoured Holcroft's derived motion as applied to the prototype 'N1' 2-6-0 and 'K1' 2-6-4T might have been used for the centre valve.

The overall engine wheelbase was 25ft 6in with overhangs of 4ft 0¾in at the front and 5ft 3in at the rear. The tender, with a 13ft 0in wheelbase equally divided, had axle loadings when full of 13t 17cwt, 14t 1cwt and 14t 10cwt, illustrative of the fact water by volume weighs more than coal. (Note that on Edward Thompson's LNER six-wheel tenders the middle axle is placed backward of centre for this very reason.) Overall length of engine and tender was 58ft 9¾in on a wheelbase of 48ft 7¼in while the overall weight in working order was 109t 10cwt.

The boiler, as already noted, came from the 'N15', though without the taper. Tube length obviously had to be reduced, from 13ft 9in to 11ft 9in though that did not appear to affect steam production. The firebox conformed to those fitted to the last series of the 'N15' with the slightly wider water legs and, therefore, marginally reduced grate area. It may be that the reduced length of the flue tubes imposed by the boiler length had a greater effect on the efficiency of the Maunsell superheater than the shorter tubes had on steaming ability. Boiler dimensions were: tubes 1604sq ft; firebox 162sq ft; superheater 283sq ft. The grate area was 28.3sq ft, its length being a comfortably managed 8ft 3½in. Pressure, as in the 'Nelson', was 220psi giving a tractive effort at 85% of that figure of 25,130lb. Compare that with the 25,320lb of an

Final BR livery for No 30935 *Sevenoaks* **was Brunswick green and black. This was likely after overhaul at Ashford in March 1958. No 30935 was one of the final survivors remaining in traffic until the end of 1962.** *G. Wheeler*

No 30910 *Merchant Taylors* in lined BR black seen in charge of the 5.5pm Cannon Street to Hastings train near Elmstead Woods, 11 May 1954. *R. C. Riley*

'Arthur' having an additional 18 tons of adhesion weight, and the need for careful handling of a 'School' when starting away becomes obvious. (Several times I saw drivers open the regulator with the engine in mid-gear and then wind the gear forward until the train moved.) The ideal adhesion factor, that is adhesion weight/tractive effort, is generally reckoned to be four. The Schools had the low one of 3.74, the Arthur 5.3. Is it any wonder the latter could walk away with 400 tons in full gear and the regulator wide open with not an atom of slip?

As to other physical dimensions, the width over the cylinders was the maximum permitted at 8ft 6½in, the boiler centre-line being 9ft 0in above the rails. From that same point the cab sides were sharply slanted inward to a width of 7ft 8in at the eaves. The maximum height overall was 13ft 0in to the chimney top. As has been noted elsewhere, occasionally with some amusement, the 'cab lights' were the 'Nelson' variety mounted upside down.

With so much of the engine incorporating readily available and proven parts, Maunsell felt confident enough to dispense with his usual practice of building a prototype and ordered 10 straight off the drawing board. Numbered 900-909, they came into traffic from Eastleigh between March and July 1930. At that time, however, the necessary upgrading of the line south of Tonbridge had not been completed so they were put to work on all three Southern sections. It was not long before enginemen were eulogising about this new 'kid on the block' and everyone was keen to get their hands on one. On the Western section particularly some quite startling work was achieved with loads of 420 tons or so being worked quite readily on schedules set out for the much more powerful

'Nelsons', though even these efforts paled against others made in the later 1930s, as we shall see.

On the Eastern section they worked the 80-minute Folkestone expresses alongside the 'L1'. S. C. Townroe maintains the 'V's were quite capable of taking nine coaches over the straight 26.4 miles between Tonbridge and Ashford in under 19 minutes, a claim repeated by Paul Drew. A railwayman author has written '[engines] non-stop through Tonbridge have been known to pass Ashford in a few seconds over 19½ minutes – an average speed of over 81½mph'. Much as I respect SCT and others I wonder if that was actually ever done. In this direction the trip is against the rising tendency of the road and the average speed required to cover the section in 19½ minutes, let alone less, exceeds the 80mph line limit in place at the time. Moreover, it begins with the rate heavily restricted by the severe 400-yard-long curve as the train enters Tonbridge. Even with steam on, the station was unlikely to be passed at much over 35mph and the train is immediately faced by a two-mile climb at 1 in 250/270/220 to Tudeley summit. I am prepared to accept this timing would be feasible in the up direction because there'd be a flying start after the 8¼ almost unbroken downhill miles to Ashford from MP64½ at Westenhanger, and the generally downhill section that follows, though there are several mini-summits *en route*. Again, however, the sharp speed restriction west of Tonbridge would require some seriously hard braking well before the station is reached. Unless someone can unearth several timings by recorders of unimpeachable reputation I think the question will remain unanswered one way or the other. But enough of argument!

It was while running on this part of the Eastern Section the stiffness of the axlebox springs in the bogie was called into question. The trackbed over the section had been built up to take heavier traffic but because there was insufficient clearance below some of the bridges over the line the track dipped beneath them. This caused the engines, with their short wheelbase and tendency to pivot vertically about the driving axle, to bounce alarmingly and to such a degree the bogie axleboxes were hitting both bottom and top stops. Stiffer springs cured the problem. Other than this the engines were absolutely right from the word go. No other modifications were required though later overhauls saw steam sanding supersede the original gravity method. In part this was to improve adhesion by getting the sand right under the wheels, but mainly it was to minimise interference with track-circuiting, particularly at termini with an uphill start away from the platforms where drivers tended to be very liberal with sand. Besides the general addition of smoke deflectors from 1932, the only other change in later batches concerned the cabside windows and cut out being raised to make lookout more comfortable for the crew. However, the early engines remained unaltered.

The naming after leading public schools may nowadays seem rather *passé* but at the time these were still held in high regard by the general public. This first 10 were naturally named after schools on Southern territory with *Eton* claiming the number one spot. The second batch of five was put into traffic in December 1932 followed by five more in May and June 1933. The last of these, No 919, was the first 'foreigner', *Harrow*. A personal interjection here. As a pre-teen on a late-1940s holiday at Westgate-on-Sea, having located the nearest newsagents I persuaded my parents I was quite capable of going on my own from our guesthouse to buy the morning paper before breakfast. That meant, timed properly, JC could gaze through the railings at the down end of the station as *Harrow* – it was always *Harrow* in my recollection, and she was a Ramsgate engine then – strode faultlessly away with her nine or ten coaches for London, that hoarse 'chittery-chattering' exhaust, as Townroe so aptly describes it, at the chimney top. Quickly crossing St Michael's Road to hang over the wall of the bridge that wonderful but quickening sound effect would come down on the breeze as No 919 got a good run at the 1 in 100 to the summit before Birchington. Ma could never understand why a trip of no more than two or three minutes often took five times as long – I had, of course, to be early enough to make sure I didn't miss the show – or that I found the station always preferable to the beach! I never missed my breakfast though.

Twelve of the forty members of the class, Nos 919-30, were named after schools outside the Southern. No 923, *Bradfield*, was originally to have been named *Uppingham* but that school objected. No other did. The final 20 engines appeared thus: Nos 920-4, Oct–Dec 1933, Nos 925-9, May–July 1934 and Nos 930-9, Dec 1934–July 1935, making 40 in all.

Performing the duty for which the class was intended, No 30909 *St Pauls* on the 'S' bend at West St Leonards whilst working a Charing Cross to Hastings service, 8 September 1951. *A. A. Selman*

As a rule the Southern made every effort to have naming ceremonies held close to the school concerned, with pupil representatives on hand for the by-then-usual photo opportunity, John Elliott's publicity machine being in full swing. Certainly this practice did the Railway's standing no harm at all. No doubt records do exist of those 'foreigners' that were treated in this way, though most were well off SR territory.

Between February 1939 and March 1941 Bulleid fitted Lemaître exhaust and large-diameter chimney to Nos 900/1/7/9/14/5/7-21/4/9-31/3/4/7-9. Nos 914 and 937 were the first, the latter also receiving an extended smokebox. In general Lemaître engines required a thicker fire though not a 'black' one, but the performance was not noticeably enhanced. Bulleid couldn't improve on perfection.

The tenders allied to Nos 910 onwards had the toolboxes and lockers fitted across the front to give added protection from the weather. In 1938 the tender of No 932, *Blundell's*, was made self-trimming with higher sides turned in to match the cab profile. But no others were so modified though this one did appear behind other class members from time to time.

Livery from the start was Olive Green with yellow and black lining. The number and 'Southern' appeared on the tender in yellow and the number appeared again on oval cast cabside plates with 'Southern Railway' in capital letters around the upper arc. The first batch had the 'E' prefix included in the number in line with the original system adopted, indicating they came under the aegis of Eastleigh. This system changed from 1931 when it was decided for simplicity's sake to add 1000 to the numbers of ex-SECR engines while the Brighton's list was upgraded by 2000. Ex-LSWR engine numbers, with a few exceptions, remained unchanged. This change also affected the numbering of continued pre-Grouping-style classes. The later builds of 'N', 'K'/'U', 'N1', 'U1', 'W' and the sole 'K1' as well as the 'L1' were numbered in the former SECR lists while the revised 'N15' and 'S15' and the completely new classes produced during the Maunsell regime – 'LN', 'V', 'Z' and 'Q' – took numbers following on from the ex-South Western list.

Excursion working for No 30915 *Brighton*. A through Kidderminster to Brighton special (hence the LMR stock) near Balcombe on a Whit Sunday, although the year was not recorded. This was another engine that lasted until the end of 1962 and was subsequently dispatched for cutting at Eastleigh. *Derek Cross*

Southern nameplates came in three sizes: up to eight letters, nine–twelve letters and thirteen letters or more. The longest of the named schools was 'KING'S-CANTERBURY' which, including the apostrophe and hyphen, counted as 17. The nameplates of the 'Saint' schools, Lawrence and Olave's, differed in that the small 't' of 'St' in the former followed the lower arc of the lettering with a full stop, but on the latter it appeared along the upper arc and without the full stop. The background to the nameplate and cabside number plate was the same vermilion red as the buffer beams though in some cases in later days black was substituted. By that time, however, Bulleid had removed the cabside plates and had the number painted here with plain 'Southern' on the tender, both in the new 'sunshine' lettering. Malachite green began to be applied from 1938. The first to receive it were Bournemouth-allocated engines Nos 925-30/2 in connection with the 'Bournemouth Limited' train, also finished in the same livery. 'Limited', as will be shown, was an indeterminate term: like its GWR London–Penzance counterpart, this train often loaded very heavily, up to 15 vehicles at times in summer. Most of the train ran no further than Bournemouth but some workings carried a Swanage portion taken on to Wareham by the front part going through to Weymouth. The 'School' heading it lodged overnight at Dorchester – that was SR territory, Weymouth was not! – in preparation for an up Weymouth–London working in the morning. The one concession made for the class was a maximum of seven coaches unassisted on Upwey bank. (The 'Arthurs' were allowed eight, the 'Nelsons', ten.)

As implied, the 'Schools' were not confined to the Hastings line even after the necessary works to bring it up to standard had been completed in July 1931. When new, Nos 900-3/5 and 6 were allocated to Dover though sub-shedded at Deal, and 904/7-9 went to Eastbourne for Brighton line duties. No 907, *Dulwich,* was the first to be fitted with smoke deflectors, in August 1931: others received them during 1932 when their value had been proven.

When all 40 were in traffic Bricklayers Arms and St Leonards obviously had the greater allocation between them, but others were at Ramsgate and Dover while 924-33 went to Fratton. The latter shed had for some time previously housed Maunsell 'U1' Moguls for Portsmouth Direct expresses but the boilers were found to be incapable of keeping up with the demand for steam over this exacting route. The 'School's had no such trouble, gambolling with gay abandon over a line that had exhausted their brethren of nominal equality. If ever there was an illustration of the falsity of 'tractive effort' as a measure of a locomotive's power it is here. (The 'U1' and the 'U' both signally failed to live up to expectations when tried experimentally over the Somerset & Dorset in 1954. The nominally less powerful 'U' was, surprisingly perhaps, reckoned the better of the two. And in contrast to the 'N' the 'U1' soon became heartily disliked west of Exeter and its stay there was correspondingly brief.) The non-stop timing for the 74½ miles from Waterloo to Portsmouth Harbour with 11 coaches was 90 minutes. But following electrification of the Portsmouth Direct in July 1937 – when the 4COR/4RES formations were allowed four minutes more! – the 'Schools' were sent to Bournemouth. As already implied, here they really showed their mettle.

Cecil J. Allen published several runs in the *Railway Magazine* of September 1939 when very substantial loads were being taken over the Bournemouth road. No 926 for example, with 14 coaches weighing 490 tons gross, reached Southampton in 92¾ minutes, including a dead stand for signals at St Denys. CJA reckoned the net time at 90½ minutes. (The headlong dash down the bank from Litchfield Box would already have been curtailed for the 20mph restriction on Northam curve.) *Repton* then reeled off the far-from-easy 28.8 miles thence to Bournemouth in 35¾ minutes start to stop. No 927 *Clifton* made an even better showing with a 15-coach train of 525 tons, being through Basingstoke (47.8 miles) over a road generally against the engine in 55½ minutes, an average of 51.6 mph start to pass, and no less than 3¾ minutes quicker than No 926. Then, taking almost a minute less to get through Winchester and with no apparent checks of significance on the way thereafter, Southampton was reached in an actual time of 88 minutes 20 seconds. South West Trains no longer operates non-stop between London and Southampton but present-day samples with, commonly, three stops – Woking, Winchester and Southampton Airport for example – are timed around 74 minutes at an average of 64.3mph, stops included. But then the four-coach Class 450 'Desiros' pack a 2,000hp punch and have 100mph capability so any comparison is rather unfair.

At the outbreak of war in 1939 not all the class had been decked in malachite though there had been a general move to 'sunshine' lettering. Black, of course, became the predominant finish until malachite reappeared in 1946. This disappeared again after Nationalisation under BR lined black, Brunswick Green not being applied to any of the engines until June 1956. Nos 900/14/19 and 32 were the only members not to receive it before overhauls ceased. This caused a tender-swap for No 932, Ashford mistakenly painting its self-trimming tender green but not the engine itself. No 905, *Tonbridge,* then receiving a green finish, took it instead. And while on the subject of tenders, Nos 912 and 921 were given ex-'LN' tenders in July and November 1961 respectively. The reason appears to have been a need for greater water capacity. The class was off the front line by that time, their duties including freight work, so provision of these tenders may have been as much about the need to stop unbraked freight trains. The 'LNs' which ceded these monsters, looking quite out of place behind the smaller engine, were Nos 854 and 865.

Allocations at Nationalisation showed the class at only four sheds with St Leonards and Bricklayers Arms still the predominant ones. Nos 900-10 were at the former and 921-3/8-39 at the latter. But Nos 911-20 at Ramsgate still took a full hand in Kent Coast workings, as did the remaining four, Nos 924-7, at Dover. Though the Ramsgate contingent worked into Victoria it appears Stewarts Lane never had an allocation, at least not regularly. Ten years on things had barely changed though there had been some swaps between sheds. The coming of the diesel-electric sets to the Hastings line, a transition completed in June 1958, and the electrification of Kent Coast services in two phases over the three years between June 1959 and June 1962, saw the class far more widespread.

No 30936 *Cranleigh* leaving Tonbridge in the summer of 1954 with the daily through train to Cannon Street via Redhill. On the extreme left it is just possible to glimpse the Eastern Section main line from London. *R. Russell*

Once more allocations appeared on the Western Section, at Nine Elms and Basingstoke, while Brighton received a substantial batch for working through to Bournemouth and Salisbury. Guildford and Redhill also featured, the few engines there presumably being principally reserved for the daily Margate–Birkenhead 'Through' service as well as other inter-Regional weekend workings to and from the Kent Coast. One train regularly headed by a 'School' from the mid-1950s was the 5.25pm London Bridge–Reading (Southern) and Tonbridge, divided at Redhill. Here was a real throwback in history to the days when the SER had use of the Brighton line from London Bridge as ordained by Parliament before its own main line via Sevenoaks opened in 1868.

Another regular duty for a Bricklayers Arms engine working home left Margate at around 2.40pm – the time varied slightly over the years – for Cannon Street. Despite having three or four coaches in its make-up this was principally a parcels and mail working. It went right round the coast via Ramsgate, Deal and Dover and then up the main line to Tonbridge, calling at most stations on the way. Thence it travelled the 'Old Road' via Godstone to Redhill and then the Brighton line, still making calls, including East Croydon and Norwood Junction, before getting back to SER territory on the 'through' part of London Bridge. There were usually two or three vans at the head of the train, convenient for Post Office staff to unload at the 'Mound'

platform opposite the up end of the original Platform 7, but now buried beneath the line alongside Platform 9. Arrival at Cannon Street was around 6.50pm though timekeeping depended quite as much on the ability of the postmen as it did on railway operating. There were no 'BRUTE' trolleys then of course: mail sacks were manhandled individually, for years usually a very swift and well organised operation.

Twenty engines had AWS fitted, if in some cases only partially, but equipping more ceased with the impending changes at the very top of the railway organisation. The British Railways Board came effectively into being on 1 January 1963 and in anticipation of this there was a move to minimise the number of steam engines transferred to it. 'School' withdrawals had begun with Nos 919 and 932 in January 1961. Thirteen more followed that year, predominantly from the Western section though Brighton saw its allocation halved. But as the end of 1962 approached the cull became a massacre. Eight went during the year including three in November, but the rest, seventeen of them, were withdrawn together in December. It was the end of an era. Though not all had been active right up to the end the sudden demise of this very fine class of engine was done with undue haste purely for political rather than operational purposes. The saving grace is, *Laus Dei,* that three have been preserved.

No 30915 was obviously a well-recorded engine! Here it is again but this time entering Bournemouth Central circa 1959, eastbound, with the stock of the through train along the coast line to its namesake town. *Neil Brayshaw*

Another Western section working, this time the return of the Saturday-only 11.43am Lymington Pier to Waterloo train seen at Southampton Central on 25 August 1962. This engine, No 30902 *Wellington*, had been allocated to Nine Elms since November 1960, having been displaced by dieselisation/electrification. The class were regular performers on the Lymington trains but, as with others, this would be its last season as it was withdrawn on 29 December 1962, after which it was stored at Nine Elms until March 1964 before being sold for scrap to Cohen's at Kettering and cut up there in April 1964. *M. J. Fox*

Somebody in high office had the good sense to see that future generations deserved the opportunity, albeit a static one then, to enjoy No 925, *Cheltenham,* now part of the National Collection. I find it ironic that it is a 'foreign' school that has been chosen as representative of Southern Railway practice. Much nearer to home No 928, *Stowe,* was purchased from BR by the National Motor Museum. It went subsequently to the East Somerset Railway and is now owned by the Maunsell Locomotive Society, who purchased it from the Motor Museum. *Stowe* is based at the Bluebell Railway along with other MLS engines, Nos 541, 847, 1618 and 1638. Many years ago I wrote that No 928 was no doubt looking forward to seeing East Grinstead again, this at a time when Horsted Keynes was still the northern limit of travel on the Bluebell and making a main line connection then seemed an impossible dream. Now, of course, it is very much a reality. What chance a main line certificate and travelling further afield?

No 926, *Repton* – another not in Southern ranks – has had just as chequered a career in preservation. This engine was among those withdrawn at the death but was then stored at Eastleigh for some time before overhaul and presentation to Steamtown in Vermont, USA. Among necessary alterations as required for operation there, *Repton* acquired a cowcatcher and bell as well as a chime whistle mounted on the dome. Buckeye couplings were also fitted and height added to the sides of the tender. She was loaned for a period to the Cape Breton Steam Railroad at Grace Bay, Canada, before returning to the UK following purchase in 1989, finding a home on the North Yorkshire Moors Railway.

Was a 'School' the finest 4-4-0 ever to work on a British railway? Some would undoubtedly argue for a Midland Compound or a North Western 'George V' or Great Western 'City', maybe a GCR 'Director'. And I recollect with considerable nostalgia the thunderous exhaust of an 'E1' lifting 10 full-and-standing bogies for Ramsgate up the 1 in 95 out of Bromley South on a Summer Saturday morning. The question can, of course, never be answered, for it is far too subjective. But few, I am sure, would argue against describing the 'V' as ranking high among the very best of the type.

Bibliography

BR Main Line Gradient Profiles, Ian Allan Ltd, in collaboration with Tothill Press, undated

Engineman SR, M. Jackman, Bradford Barton. Undated

Footplate over The Mendips, Peter Smith, OPC, 1978

Historic Locomotive Drawings in 4mm Scale, F. J. Roche, Ian Allan Ltd, undated (drawings all dated 1948)

Lawson Billinton, A Career Cut Short, Klaus Marx, The Oakwood Press, 2007

Locomotives Illustrated No 2, The Schools, Paul Drew, Ian Allan Ltd, 1975

Locomotives Illustrated No 78, Maunsell SR 4-4-0s, Chris Leigh, Ian Allan Ltd, 1991

Maunsell Locomotives, Brian Haresnape, Ian Allan Ltd, 1977.

Nameplates of the Big Four, Frank Burridge, OPC, 1975

Railway Track Diagrams No 5, Southern & TfL, Ed. by Gerald Jacobs, TRACKmaps, 3rd edition, 2008

Richard Maunsell, An Engineering Biography, J. E. Chacksfield, The Oakwood Press, 1998

Sir Herbert Walker's Southern Railway, C. F. Klapper, Ian Allan Ltd, 1973

The Arthurs, Nelsons and Schools of the Southern, S. C. Townroe, Ian Allan Ltd, 1973

The South Eastern & Chatham Railway, O. S. Nock, Ian Allan Ltd, 1961

TRACKatlas of Mainland Britain, 2009

Wainwright and his Locomotives, Klaus Marx, Ian Allan Ltd, 1985

'Steamindex.com' provided much information about Thomas 'Jock' Finlayson. Several websites have been consulted to do with the origins of the Maunsell name and for other corroborative evidence.

The reader is also referred specifically to *Southern Way* issues Nos 2 (illustration of a 'Schools' class engine with cab ARP protection) and No 8 (article on the renaming of *Uppingham* to *Bradfield*.)

No 30925 *Cheltenham* preserved as part of the National Collection seen here during a repose at Tyseley – note the preserved LSWR 'T9' behind. Following withdrawal from Basingstoke shed in December 1962, the engine – along with others also subject to 'official preservation' – spent some time stored at various locations before a permanent home could be found. *A. J. Lambert*

The
Southern Way

The regular volume for the Southern devotee
MOST RECENT BACK ISSUES

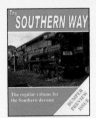

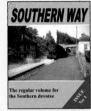

The Southern Way is available from all good book sellers, or in case of difficulty, direct from the publisher. (Post free UK) Each regular issue contains at least 96 pages including colour content.

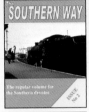

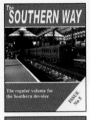

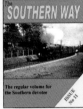

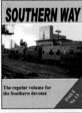
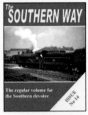
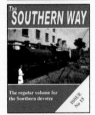

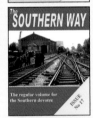
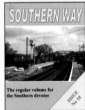

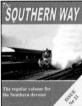
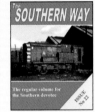

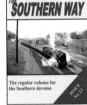
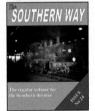
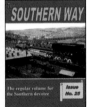
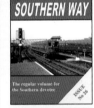
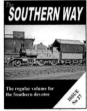

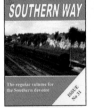

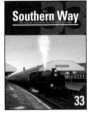
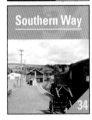
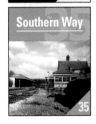
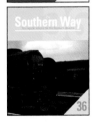

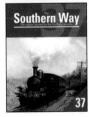
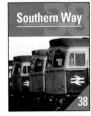

£11.95 each
£12.95 from Issue 7
£14.50 from Issue 21
£14.95 from Issue 35

Subscription for four
issues available
(Post free in the UK)
www.crecy.co.uk